Trekking Peru:

A Hiking Guide to Independent Travel

Andy Fine

andyfineadventure@gmail.com

Cover by Andy Fine

Photos by Andy Fine

Trekking Peru: A Hiking Guide for Independent Travel

Second Edition: 2023

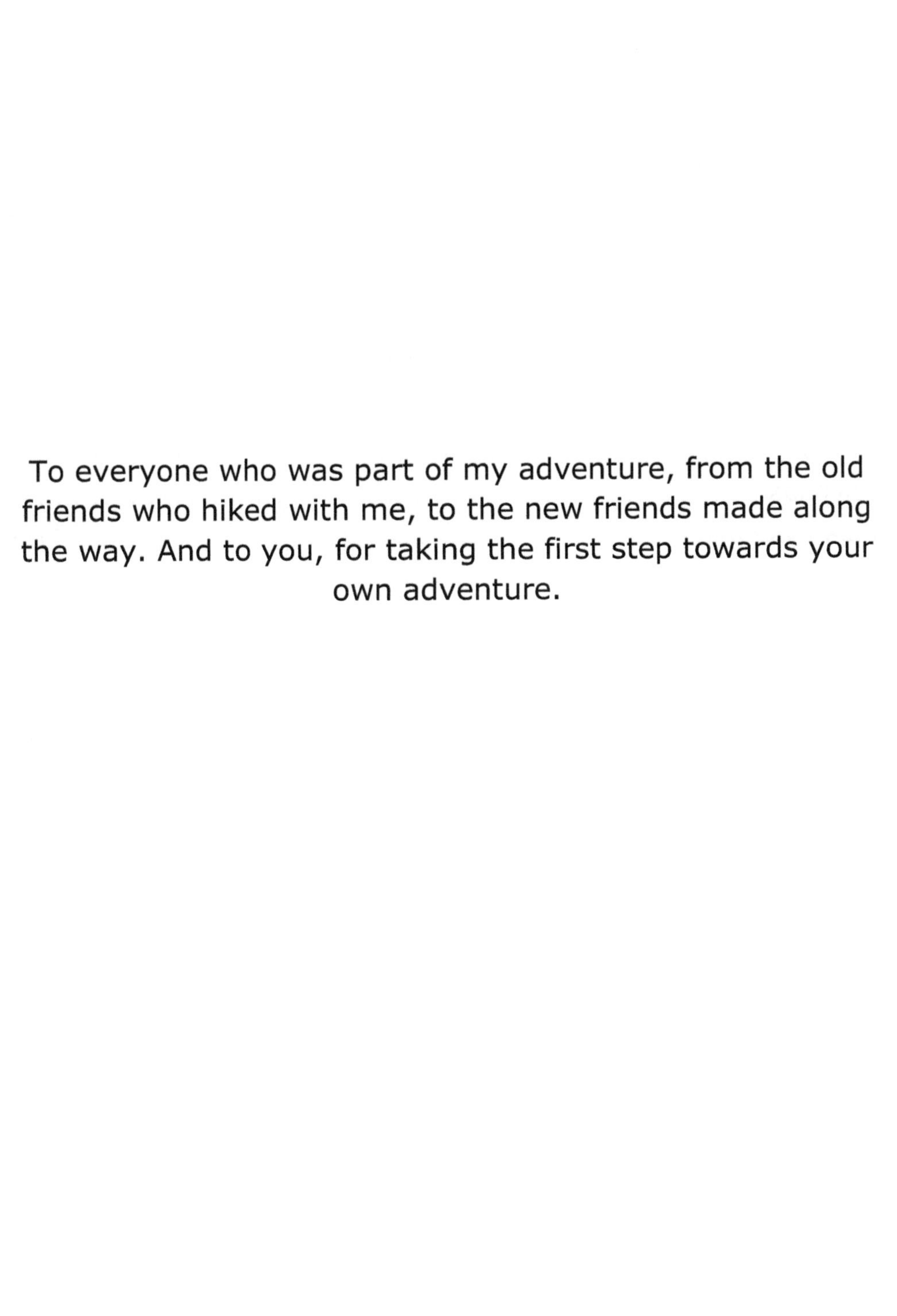

To everyone who was part of my adventure, from the old friends who hiked with me, to the new friends made along the way. And to you, for taking the first step towards your own adventure.

Table of Contents

Introduction

The world is now smaller than ever. Traveling from one corner of the globe to the other has never been more accessible and economical. The opportunities for anyone with a passport to venture to a foreign land and experience something completely new are limitless. Yet, even as destinations become easier to reach, those with an adventurous spirit can still find hidden oases if they are willing to step out of their comfort zone, know how to ask the right questions, and seek out the most help and knowledge.

Peru is one of the most traveled to places in South America. The diverse landscape, delicious cuisine, and the infamous Machu Picchu bring visitors here from all over the globe. There is something for everyone here. For me, it was the pristine mountains of the Andes and the epic trekking opportunities that lured me to travel for two months. From the Huayhuash Circuit of the Cordillera Blanca to Cusco's neighboring Ausangate, trekking throughout Peru is nothing short of spectacular and needs to be on every backpacker's bucket list.

"Trekking Peru" is designed for those travelers who crave that rush of adrenaline that comes from reaching the summit of a high mountain pass with jaw-dropping views and the sense of peace that flows through the soul from the sound of a rushing river miles from the nearest electrical outlet. It's also intended for that particular breed of adventurer who feels the most significant level of satisfaction and accomplishment when these feelings are derived from demanding physical and mental trials. Every hike described herein is not for the faint-hearted. Each requires a genuine comfort with the wilderness and ability to face all the challenges it presents. This guidebook will provide you with the requisite knowledge to independently hike some of Peru's most popular, and some of its lesser-known treks *without the reliance on a tour company*. My goal is to give you the practical information every seasoned hiker seeks when they plan a trek to a new place. Additional resources will certainly complement this guide to fill in the ancillary details like restaurants and city lodging necessary for your complete trip planning. This guide includes thorough information on the following Peruvian treks:

- Salkantay Trek
- Ausangate/Rainbow Mountain Trek
- Huayhuash Circuit
- Alpamayo Circuit
- Laguna Parón
- Laguna 69
- Volcán Chachani

My two months of trekking and traveling in Peru was an absolute dream. Soaring mountains, hypnotic turquoise lakes, and vast glaciers completely satisfied the monster inside me that so desperately hungers for adventure. Not only did I have the privilege to hike amongst these giants, but I did so for considerably less money than you might think and had the solitude and flexibility that only hiking independently without a structured guided tour provides. After two years since my original trip, I returned to Peru to hike the mighty Huayhuash Circuit again. The second edition of this book includes a few revised recommendations and updates on some logistical details including costs, and alternative exits to the trail.

Trekking independently has clear advantages over hiking with a structured guided tour group. Having the freedom and complete control over where and when I go is important to me. It is also almost always far cheaper to travel independently. However, it would not be fair nor responsible not to mention what hiking throughout the Peruvian Andes alone also entails. Without a structured tour guide, logistics, transportation, and safety are all in your hands. You'll have to take on the role of a Peruvian donkey and haul all your gear and the food you need on your back. For those that are used to heavy packs and are shrugging this off, consider that you will be completing these hikes at altitudes you perhaps have not reached yet. Despite these challenges, those with the right hiking experience and willingness to conquer physically demanding hikes can do everything listed in this book independently.

Two months provided me with a lot of experience trekking in this area, but there are still more hidden gems to explore that other references can assist with. I genuinely hope that this guidebook is a useful reference both in your pre-trip planning process and while you are executing your adventure. Please accept my invitation to contact me with any questions or provide feedback at andyfineadventure@gmail.com.

Trail conditions, bus routes, and other factors impacting the trail change over time. If you encounter any inaccuracies, please do not hesitate to contact me so that I may provide updated information to others in the future. Thank you, and congratulations on selecting Peru for your upcoming adventure.

Pre-Trip Planning

Peru Overview Map

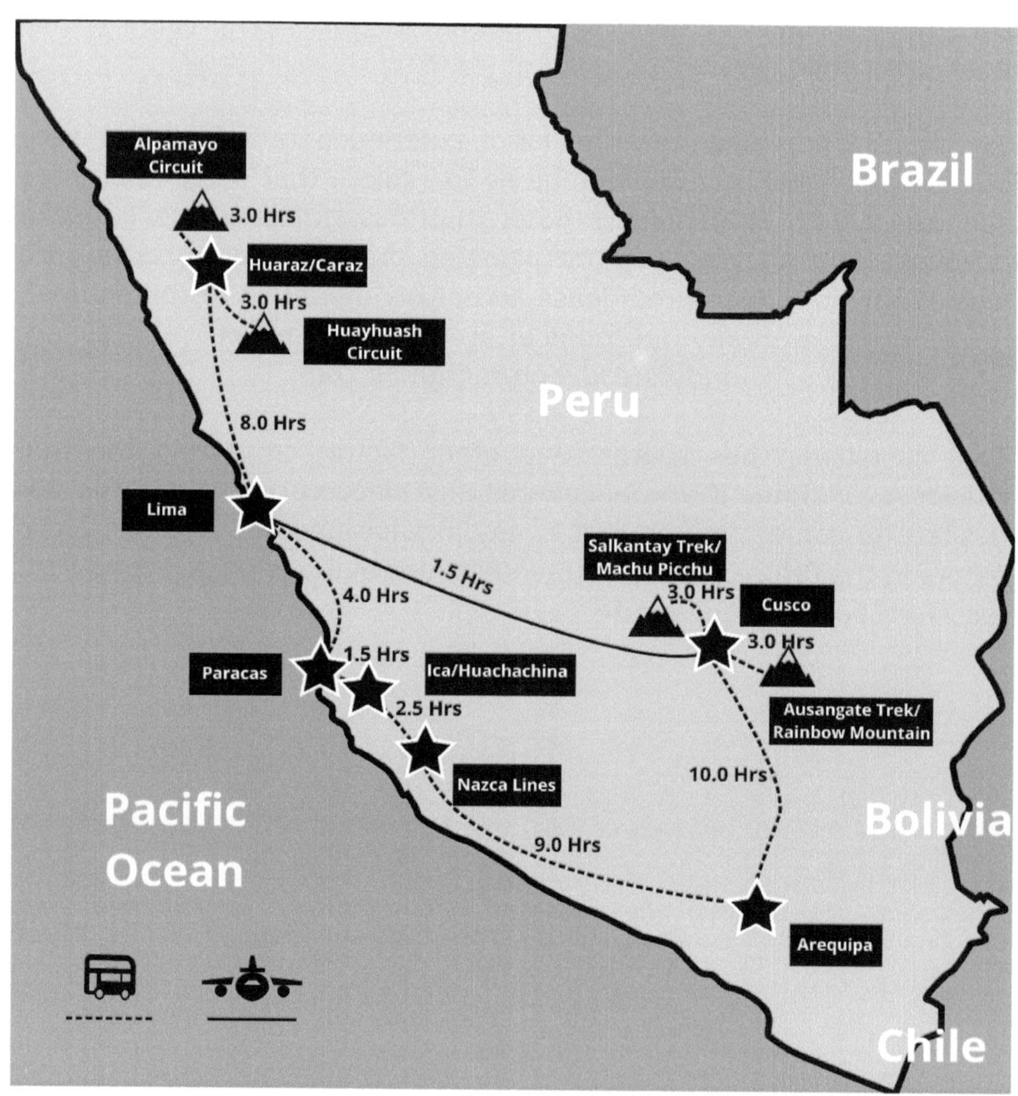

Peru Introduction

Peru is located on the western side of South America, north of Chile and south of Ecuador. It provides every traveler the opportunity to experience something wild. The vast diversity of landscapes throughout the country draws bird watchers to its Amazon, lovers of history to its ancient ruins, and trekkers to its Andes mountains. Hiking throughout Peru is incredibly unique. It is rare to find terrain so spectacular but not yet tainted by commercialization and profit-driven exploitations of nature.

The lack of development in the various Peruvian treks provides the nomadic traveler specific advantages. There are few trail signs anywhere; no signs patting you on the back saying you made it to the top so take a picture. At the time of this writing, the only trail that requires advanced reservations and permits is the Inca Trail. This top-rated trek leads to Machu Picchu and requires reservations at least six months of advanced. Only on the Inca Trail will you find anything resembling a Park Ranger or other authoritative figure. Having the flexibility to make changes to our daily itinerary on the spot was very helpful compared to the process of reserving campsites in advance for example in Patagonia's Torres del Paine National Park.

Acclimatizing

It is necessary to include ample time for acclimatizing to the high elevation before beginning any Peruvian hike. Most treks throughout the region range from 12,000 to as high as 17,000 feet. No matter from where you are flying in, I recommend dedicating a minimum of 48 hours in the nearest town to the trailhead before embarking up into the mountains. My adventure began in the Cusco region of Peru. At over 11,000 feet in Cusco my body could feel the physical symptoms of being at such a high elevation. My recommendation is to allow two full days after you arrive in Peru before beginning any trek. Especially if you plan to hike independently, you need the time for your body to adjust before carrying a full pack at high altitude. One full day to acclimatize might be okay, but only if you have ample experience with high altitude trekking. It is better to overestimate the amount of time necessary to acclimatize because every person will respond physiologically differently from the change in elevation.

Altitude sickness is a risk faced by all trekkers and needs to be taken seriously. This dangerous condition can be prevented by being in tune with what your body is telling you, drinking plenty of water, and medications including Diamox prescribed by a doctor. At higher elevations, perspiration evaporates more rapidly making it difficult to regulate water levels. Drink at least an extra one to two liters of water per day more than at sea level. Avoid alcohol consumption during your acclimatizing period. Just two drinks are enough to depress breathing at high elevation and cause lower blood oxygen.

At over 10,000 feet, it is recommended to not gain more than 1,500 feet from sleeping locations. Also, sleeping more than 1,000 feet below the highest point will also help because slow automatic breathing during sleep reduces oxygen consumption. Take ascents slowly with periodic breaks to allow your body to adjust to the changing elevation. As long as you listen to your body and have the wisdom to stop or descend when these symptoms become apparent, you should be just fine. Before each day, you should know the overall topography of your route. Every trail map included in this guide contains elevations of critical points to help give you an idea of how much ascent there is. Use this information to pace your climbs to help avoid altitude sickness. The fastest remedy to altitude sickness is also the simplest: descend to a lower elevation. Do not let pride and stubbornness threaten your health; it is not worth it.

Proper physical preparation will also help combat the risk of altitude sickness. As soon as you reach 5,000 feet, your body begins to recognize the reduction in oxygen levels and responds by increasing heart rates and respirations. Commit to getting in prime cardiovascular fitness at VO2 Max, a measure of the body's oxygen consumption through some high intensity interval training. In addition to less oxygen, higher altitudes also bring increased ultraviolet radiation. Wear UPF 50+ clothing and cover any exposed skin with sunscreen that is at least SPF 30 and protects against UVA and UVB.

Transportation

Buses dominate the transportation industry in Peru. Peru is a mountainous country where trains are not present except in the case of getting to Machu Picchu. There are three reputable companies that offer á la carte bus tickets: Cruz del Sur, Oltursa, and Movil Bus. In some cases, local bus companies provide the same ride; however, I recommend sticking with the big three as much as possible. The safety and comfort provided by these companies are worth the slightly higher cost, especially on rides in Peru that can last more than fifteen hours! Of the three, Cruz del Sur was the highest cost and most luxurious option. I was delighted with my experience using all three companies, so choose whichever offers the best time of departure for your plan and at the best cost. Download their mobile apps for secure ticket purchasing.

Another transportation option to consider is PeruHop. This bus package company offers a bundle deal which might be a cheaper and easier solution if you plan on circumnavigating around the country. The basic idea is that you can hop on the bus at one of their terminals and get off at any other point along the route. You pay more the more segments you take. I generally don't recommend these bundle packages because they can be limiting on the destinations you can visit and when. Having the flexibility to make my plan as I go fits my travel style and personality better. But I certainly can see the package deal being something worth investigating for the right traveler who would enjoy the social community gained by traveling in a more collaborative environment.

Depending on where you are traveling, flying might be a much better option than a bus. It will be more expensive to fly, but specific itineraries will take an exorbitant amount of time on the ground compared to the air. It takes much longer to drive anywhere than you would anticipate by looking at a map because the mountains add many extra miles compared to how the crow flies. Trips requiring an eighteen-hour bus ride might be made with a ninety-minute plane ride. Several local airlines offer domestic flights. My experiences with LATAM and Sky Airlines were both above my expectations.

Within the cities themselves, you will find plenty of taxis and bicycle drivers. There is a golden rule of traveling applicable in most parts of the world: ensure that you negotiate and agree on a fare BEFORE departing for your destination. This is especially true in Peru where none of the taxis has meters. If you don't predetermine a price, you risk the danger of a driver fighting with you for an unreasonable fare. Cusco and Lima both had complicated city bus systems that are an option if your budget is extra tight. Uber is a popular option as well in Lima. For each trek in this guidebook, I will outline my recommended transportation route to arrive at the trailhead. These typically involve a bus that looks like a large passenger van, or as they are usually referred to, *collectivos*.

Trip Duration and Recommended Itineraries

Peru is such a diverse country with endless trails to hike, history to explore, and food to enjoy that you could easily be entertained for as long as you can afford. If you intend to complete any of the hikes in this guide, you need to plan at least eight to ten days in the country as a minimum. Two full days of acclimatizing time should be included in your itinerary. Everyone will have different circumstances in their life that will dictate how much time you can spend in Peru. Spending less than a week wouldn't allow you to complete any of the multi-day treks, but you could still experience the main attractions like Machu Picchu and Lima.

Part of your itinerary plan will have to include days for transportation and rest before pursuing the next challenge. Here I will outline a few sample itineraries I would recommend for some standard trip durations. They each solely focus on trekking activities. Other complementary guide resources will help you if you want to add different activities into your trip. These itineraries are designed for those looking to fit as much trekking into the adventure as possible.

Trek Durations

Salkantay Trek: 4-5 Nights
Ausangate Trek: 5-6 Nights
Huayhuash Circuit: 6-10 Nights
Alpamayo Circuit: 9-10 Nights

10 Days in Peru – Salkantay Trek/Machu Picchu

Day 1: Arrive in Cusco
Day 2-3: Acclimatize in Cusco
Day 4-8: Complete Salkantay Trek
Day 9: Visit Machu Picchu, take the train back to Cusco
Day 10: Depart Cusco

15 Days in Peru Option 1: Salkantay/Machu Picchu and Ausangate Treks

Day 1: Arrive in Cusco
Day 2-3: Acclimatize in Cusco
Day 4-8: Complete Salkantay Trek
Day 9: Visit Machu Picchu, take the train back to Cusco
Day 10-14: Ausangate Trek
Day 15: Depart Cusco

30 Days in Peru – Salkantay/Machu Picchu, Ausangate, and Huayhuash Circuit

Day 1: Arrive in Cusco
Day 2-3: Acclimatize in Cusco
Day 4-8: Complete Salkantay Trek
Day 9: Visit Machu Picchu,bus to Cusco
Day 10: Day in Cusco
Day 11-15: Ausangate Trek
Day 16: Day in Cusco
Day 17: Fly to Lima, Bus to Huaraz
Day 18-19: Day in Huaraz
Day 20-30: Huayhuash Circuit, bus to Lima

15 Days in Peru Option 2: Only Huayhuash Circuit

Day 1: Arrive in Lima, Overnight bus to Huaraz
Day 2-3: Huaraz trek prep
Day 4-14: Huayhuash Circuit, bus to Lima
Day 15: Depart Lima

24 Days in Peru – Salkantay/Machu Picchu and Huayhuash Circuit

Day 1: Arrive in Cusco
Day 2-3: Acclimatize in Cusco
Day 4-8: Complete Salkantay Trek
Day 9: Visit Machu Picchu, take the train back to Cusco
Day 10: Fly to Lima, Bus to Huaraz
Day 11-12: Day in Huaraz
Day 13-23: Huayhuash Circuit, bus to Lima
Day 24: Depart Lima

Six Weeks in Peru – Salkantay, Ausangate, Huayhuash, and Alpamayo Circuit

See 30 Day recommended itinerary up until Day 30.
Day 31-41: Alpamayo Circuit
Day 42: Rest Day in Huaraz, bus to Lima
Day 43: Day in Lima
Day 44: Depart Lima

Money

Before visiting any new country, you must have a thorough understanding of the local currency and standard methods of payment so that you avoid scams and being taken advantage of. There is nothing a vendor likes more than a tourist fumbling through bills they do not understand nor have a grasp of what the bills are worth in their home currency. Peru's currency is named the Peruvian Sol and is inflated compared to the US Dollar currently at about 3.3x. Coins come in increments of 1, 2, and 5 soles as well as reasonably worthless coins called *centiminos*. Paper currency comes in increments of 10, 20, 50, and 100 soles. A 10 soles bill is going to be worth about $3.30, a 50 soles bill worth about $16 and so on. Check the current exchange rates before departing to Peru and make sure you have a good grasp of what each bill and coin is generally worth. I also recommend purchasing a few days' supply of Peruvian currency from your local bank before beginning your travels in case the local ATMs malfunction or your cards get rejected. Make sure to alert your bank and credit card companies of your travel plans.

You will find that most establishments will accept credit cards (Visa was most popular), but frequently there is a 5% surcharge. For more substantial expenses like hotels, hostels and restaurants, I generally prefer credit card payments over cash because I would rather have the miles earned with my credit card and the security of the purchase. Knowing the policies and fees on your credit cards and ATMs will dictate the best way for you to spend money. Travel credit cards with your preferred airline are a great way to accumulate rewards for travel and to save on foreign transaction fees. In general, if you can use a travel credit card with no charge or transaction fee, do it. The credit card likely has a better conversion rate compared to what you will get from a foreign bank's ATM. Even many of the tourist markets where you would not anticipate vendors accepting credit cards will take them, but they will not give you as good a discounted price and only will accept it if you are making a significant purchase.

ATMs are abundant throughout the main cities of Cusco and Lima, but as soon as you venture out towards the treks in the rural towns you will struggle to find an ATM, and everything is paid for with cash. Make sure that you have ample amounts of money to cover both expected and unexpected expenses you will encounter. Every bank has different maximum withdrawals they will allow from their ATM. The most common withdrawal maximum is 400 soles. I recommend using the Banco de Credito del Peru (BCP) for all your cash needs because they have a relatively small transaction fee and allow you to withdraw 700 soles at once. This limits the overall foreign transaction fee you will incur for every sol you withdraw.

Language

Spanish is the dominant and official language spoken throughout Peru. As you dive deeper into the depths of the Inca Valley and other remote regions, there are indigenous dialects that have Spanish similarities, but each with its variations and distinctions. Before traveling to Peru, you need to become acquainted with at least basic terminology and phrases applicable to traveling and trekking throughout Peru. However, there is an enormous spread between communicating with people in a foreign country and speaking the language. My foreign language skills are honestly quite poor, but I was able to successfully get by with just some basic knowledge and help from apps like Yandex Translation. The language barrier is not large enough for English speakers to be threatened by, but still, invest in learning as much Spanish as you can. The real reward of speaking the language is not the ability to ask for help and get directions, but to connect with the locals on a deeper level and truly get acquainted with their culture. Making an effort to talk with the locals in their native language reduces the "take it and leave it" culture that can arise in the travel community.

At a minimum for any journey, your Spanish vocabulary must include frequent numbers, greetings, everyday food items, navigational directions, leading questions like "where is," "how much," and most importantly, please and thank you. To prepare, you can use free language learning apps like Duolingo or more advanced paid applications such as Babel. At a minimum when traveling in a country with another language begin with saying "hello, do you speak English" in their language. This shows respect and you will be amazed at how helpful this approach can be.

Wildlife

Peru's high altitude limits the diversity of wildlife you will likely experience throughout your journey. Over two months of backpacking in the region, the only wildlife I encountered at high elevation were large foxes and the occasional condor. But that is not to say you won't see any other animals. Throughout the many treks, you will undoubtedly find collections of grazing animals owned by local farmers but travel far from home each day. Llamas, alpacas, cows, sheep, horses, and dogs will be frequent companions along the trek. Dogs will frequently walk alongside you for days at a time. They have played the game many times, tricking tourists into feeding them all their delicious trail snacks. I highly recommend refraining from making these dogs your surrogate for the pet you left at home. These are wild animals and can become aggressive when denied what they want. They are best left alone. Do not get too close to the grazing cows and horses as they can also behave erratically and aggressively. The positive news is that you do not need to be highly concerned about the safety of your food overnight. Each night, all of my food was kept inside my pack under the tent vestibule and was never stolen by critters or larger hunters.

When To Go, Weather

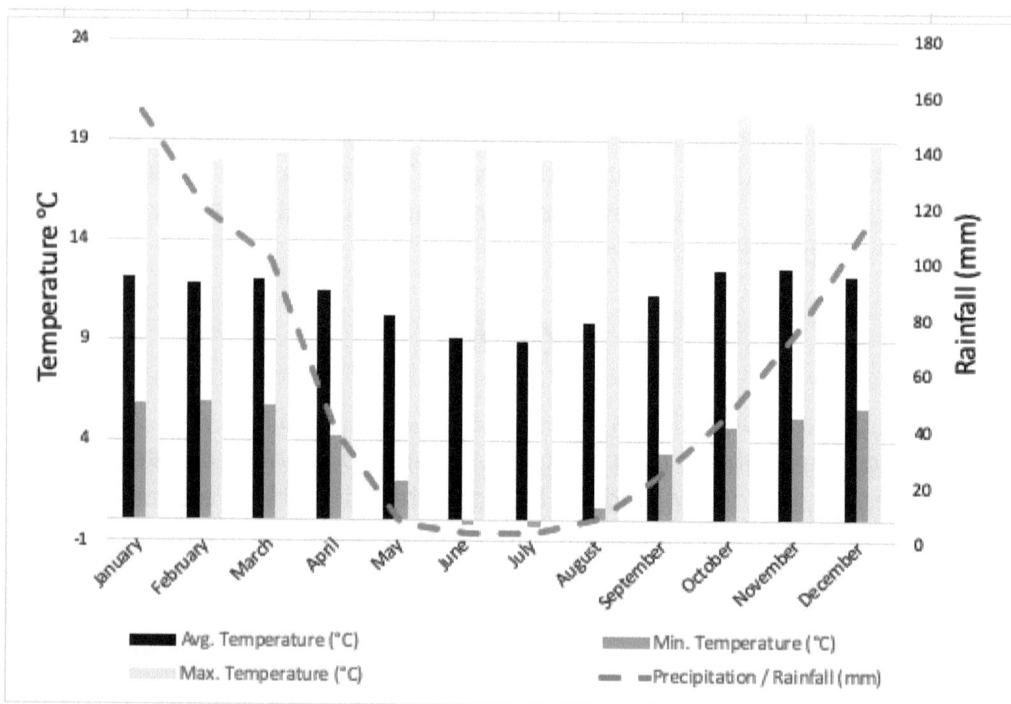

"Data.org." Climate, https://en.climate-data.org/south-america/peru/cusco/cusco-1016/

Above you'll find weather data gathered for Cusco, Peru. Weather in Cusco will be a pretty good benchmark for the weather you can expect on the treks listed in this guide. The rainy season in Peru lasts from the end of September to early April. The best time to trek Peru is during the dry season of mid-May to August. You will encounter the highest number of like-minded tourists during this time of year, but the optimal weather is worth the sacrifice of solitude.

Throughout two months of trekking from mid-May to mid-July, the weather was truly spectacular. The days were filled with perfect blue-sky and comfortable hiking temperatures around 18°C. The same cannot be said about the night. As soon as dusk arrives, there is a dramatic drop in temperature that will inevitably force you into every warm layer. Nights in the mountains of Peru are extreme and will be shocking for anyone who has not camped in sub-freezing temperatures before. Certain nights caused my boots and Camelbak bladder to freeze when mistakenly left outside the tent. However, with the proper gear, the cold will be your friend. The complete absence of bugs in these mountains is due to the high altitude and the cold nights. I'll take cold nights for no bugs any day.

In addition to temperature and rainfall, trekkers in Peru should also be aware of the typical sunrise and sunset times. These times will be important in deciding a wake-up time and pacing out the trek. Since Peru is in the southern hemisphere, the prime hiking months of May-August are actually during its winter season. Winter brings the shortest days of sunlight in the year. Typical days during the peak season will have a sunrise between 05:30 and 06:00, and sunset will be around 17:30-18:00. This early sunset was astonishing upon our first days of trekking. Early sunset rigorously dictated our hiking schedule each day. To maintain our daily goal of arriving at the campsite 1.5-2 hours before sunset, this meant starting hiking by 07:30 and arriving at the site by 15:30.

Required Documentation

Peru is an open-door country with limited requirements to enter the country. For most American and Western European citizens, there is no tourist visa required. The maximum duration of stay that will be granted by immigration is 183 days. *** Critical note! This does not necessarily mean that the immigration officer will grant you this maximum visa duration upon arrival. I wrongly assumed that my visa issued when I arrived in Cusco was for 183 days. Only upon my departure from Lima two months later was I informed that I was only given a visa for thirty days. I thus had to incur a charge based on the number of days I overstayed my visa limitation.

In hindsight, this was likely my own fault when I went through customs. I probably did not understand the officer when he asked me about my plans for Peru. *My advice is for you to be extra clear with the immigration officer when you initially go through customs, telling him/her how long you are planning on traveling through the country.* If you plan on spending more than thirty days, make sure they understand and grant you the correct amount of days. The number of days you are issued is printed on your passport stamp.

Required Reservations

A significant perk to trekking in Peru is that you do not need to deal with frustrating and limiting campsite reservation processes. The only activities that require advanced reservations are permits for the Inca Trail and entrance tickets to Machu Picchu. All of the treks detailed in this guide were completed independently with no advanced reservations. Having the flexibility to modify an itinerary without the constraints of a permit dictating where and when you need to be is a huge advantage.

Packing List

Required gear will be different to each individual, but here are some general tips and guidelines for the equipment you will need:

Do not overpack. More likely than not, you will bring too much "stuff." Every ounce you pack is another ounce you have to carry on your back. Remember, the mass majority of hikers completing these treks are doing so with a chartered guide and donkeys to carry gear, and for good reason. These hikes are challenging even without a full pack. If you are planning on following this guide and trekking independently, limiting your pack weight will be extremely important. Packing is always a process for me. When my pack is full of the items I've selected, I then take items out until the bag is only 75-80% full. This strategy always has worked out since I like to buy things as I go and need the room at the end to bring them back. An exception to this rule is if I am bringing food, as that is space I will gain back throughout the trip.

When traveling with a group, "group gear" is anything that the whole group shares such as cooking supplies, food, tents, and water purification. Make sure that you divide out group gear evenly so that weight is well distributed. Keep this group gear assignment constant throughout the trip so that you always know where to find each item. Before you leave on your trip, have everyone bring their gear to one location, then unpack and repack together. This eliminates unnecessary duplicates and may help you realize that everyone thought someone else was bringing something that no one has packed. It is also the best way and time to divide up group gear and food evenly.

Use these as examples, but your own needs will dictate which product is right for you. If you are traveling to Peru, you likely have done some hiking before and have much of the equipment listed already. Below is an explanation for those that might not have purchased the necessary items previously. For female adventurers, use the items I've provided as a starting point and supplement/exchange as needed.

Camping Gear

- **Backpack.** Selecting a pack will be one of the largest and, therefore, one of the most important investments you make. Having a pack that is the right size for your body and amount of gear you need will severely impact your comfort on the trail.

Packs are sized by volume; I recommend the Gregory Baltoro 75L Pack if you plan on going on extended hikes such as the Huayhuash and Alpamayo Circuits; if not a 65L could be sufficient. When selecting a pack, make sure it has high-quality materials and features, particularly the waist belt padding and compartments that offer easy access to gear when the pack is on your back. Any quality camping store such as REI will be able to help you select the best pack for you.

- **Camping Stove.** I own an MSR Dragonfly Stove, which is a bit larger than other units but gives you the best performance and versatility in cooking options. If you have an MSR stove, we found white gas,_*"Bencina Blanca,"* at different outfitters and hardware stores *"ferreterías"* in Cusco and Huaraz. The majority of people we encountered used stoves like Jetboils, which use pressurized canisters easily found throughout the area. These are great if you are only using the stove to boil water because they are more compact and economical.
- **Cookware.** Bring cookware that is best suited for your selected stove and what you intend to cook. I love my Light My Fire Mess Kit.
- **Sleeping Pad.** I used to think that people who use these weren't as rugged as I am. But the truth is sleeping pads are essential only partially because of comfort; their primary purpose is warmth. Having a layer of air between the ground and your body severely limits the conduction of cold air while you sleep. I use the Nemo Tensor for its superior warmth, compact design, and easy fill bag for inflating.
- **Sleeping Bag.** If you have a poor-quality sleeping bag, you will regret not upgrading. Peruvian nights are really cold; one night it snowed! Invest in a quality bag that has at least a 20°F rating. Sleeping bags come in either synthetic material or down. Down will generally be lighter and more compact but can be challenging to deal with if it gets wet.

- **Tent.** Although it is possible to rent tents in various cities like Cusco and Huaraz, it is a good investment to purchase a quality tent. Two key features that I look for in a standard two-person tent is access (get one with two doors so each person can get in independently) and wind/rain protection. If your group has more than two people, I recommend having multiple two-person tents instead of purchasing one larger one. A three-person tent would be the largest option for backpacking. Four-person tents are cumbersome to the point that they will be too much of a burden on whoever gets stuck carrying it. Bring extra stakes so you can stake out the rainfly both perpendicularly and in line with the poles, as well as the corners of your tent (8 total). I've been happy with my REI Half Dome 2 Plus for years now. ** Pro-tip: If you need to distribute weight between members of the group, have one person carry the tent and the other the poles.
- **Trekking Poles.** Peru was my first trip using trekking poles. I am now an absolute believer in the value they bring to a hike. The main benefits of trekking poles include balance and limiting the impact on your lower body. I genuinely could not believe how my body was still feeling strong and knee pain-free even after weeks of high impact. They are indeed worth the investment. There is a wide range of options for trekking poles made of different materials and at a variety of pricepoints. I found my mid-grade poles were not too heavy even after two months of use. So only spend a premium on poles if weight is an essential factor for you.
- **Water Filtration.** It is imperative to filter all water found on the trails because of the livestock that graze throughout the area. Most water filtration processes involve either chemical or physical separation. I recommend MSR's Autoflow Gravity Filtration Bag, which allows you to filter a large quantity of water with gravity as your source of energy. The downside with this

option is the size. Each choice has its pros and cons; it all depends on what priorities you have.

- **Camelbak Bladder and Nalgene**. It also is a good idea to bring a spare mouthpiece for your Camelbak just in case.
- **Poop Kit.** Yes, everyone poops, especially on the trail. On the trail, follow Leave No Trace principles. This includes burying solid waste in a dug hole 100 ft away from the trail and 200 ft from a water source. REI sells Sanitation Trowels that work well and are lightweight. Pack a small container of hand sanitizer and toilet paper as well.
- **Clothesline.** I always bring about 50 feet of thin rope to use as a clothesline, knowing it can also help in an emergency situation.
- **GPS Device.** Peru was the first trip that I used my new Garmin inReach. They are expensive, running at $450 plus a monthly data plan ranging from $15-$100 a month. But if you are trekking independently in this extremely remote terrain, it is worth every penny. This device has satellite communication capabilities so you can send out text messages checking in with friends and family or to first responders in case of an emergency miles from the nearest cell tower. My family loved having the peace of mind knowing that I was safe each day of my journey. I would not have taken the eleven-day Alpamayo Circuit by myself without the ability to contact safety personnel in the event of an emergency. You can't put a price tag on safety.

Clothing

Peru will have you continually playing the "Game of Layers." Most days you would find me hiking in shorts and a long sleeve base layer. But then as soon as dusk encroaches on the day, I'm bracing for full subfreezing conditions. Layers will allow you to adjust to the various temperatures you encounter. It is impressive how different your body feels when you are hiking compared to stagnation. Typical mornings start with all layers on, but as you start walking, your heart rate goes up and off go the layers. Then stopping for any short period and the cold wind will tell you to put them back on. You only need enough clothes for each individual trek because you can do laundry in any of the cities between treks.

- **Rain Gear.** This includes a quality rain jacket, rain pants, and a rain cover for your pack. Even though during peak season it is rare to hike in the rain, they double as excellent protection from the high winds you will undoubtedly experience. They will be precious pieces of equipment on your trip. *Invest in quality rain gear.* Cheaper rain gear loses its water resistance over time! Many packs now come with a rain cover, but purchase separately, if necessary.
- **Hiking Boots.** Hiking boots are another one of the most essential pieces of gear for you on the trail. A high-quality hiking boot will be waterproof and feel stable with a rigid structure that prevents ankle rolls and most importantly, must fit you. Wear them on a couple of day hikes to see how well they fit your feet and if you feel any hot spots. Salomon's Quest 4D was fantastic.
- 2-3 Synthetic, Non-Cotton T-Shirts
- 1 Lightweight Zip Off Trail Pants. Best ones can be removed with your boots still on!
- 2 Long Sleeve Synthetic Layers
- 1 Thermal Long Underwear
- 1 Down Thermal Layer
- 5-7 Hiking Socks
- 2-3 Hiking Underwear
- Lightweight Synthetic Gloves
- Warm Winter Hat. However, you can find lovely warm hats in the tourist markets that might be more fun to use than one from home.
- Baseball cap for sun protection.

- Site shoes such as Chacos or throw away sneakers. AKA something you can wear when you arrive at a campsite, you'll want to get out of the boots!
- ** Pro-tip: If you are renting a car, you'll have a place to store stuff while you are out hiking. Bring some comfy clothes for car rides that you wouldn't usually take on the trail and maybe even a clean set of clothes for the journey home that you leave in the car throughout the trip.

Miscellaneous Gear

- Travel Documentation
    - Valid Passport. ** Pro-tip: In addition to bringing your passport, bring a photocopy of it, upload a scanned copy to the cloud and send to a friend or family member back home. If you lose your passport, it is much easier to get it replaced abroad if you can provide a copy.
    - Printed copies of all reservations including campsites, hostels, rental car, travel insurance, etc.

    - Headlamp
    - Toiletries (including any medications you might need)
    - Pack Towel
    - Polarized Sunglasses
    - Travel Journal. Great waterproof paper products exist to protect your journal from the elements.
    - Multi-tool
    - Camera and Camera Tripod
    - Duct Tape **Pro-tip: Take a Nalgene and wrap it in layers of duct tape so you don't have to take the whole roll. Saves space!
    - Padlock for hostels
    - Power Bank
    - Compactable Daypack
    - Camping Pillow – Optional, I typically use clothes bag as a pillow to save space.
    - Sleeping Mask
- Playing Cards
- All-Purpose Wash Soap
- 2 Carabiners to hang items from pack
- 4 Bandanas – use for cleaning and first aid
- First Aid Supplies. At a minimum, any good trekking first aid kit will include the following:
    - Foot care products: Moleskin, Band-Aids
    - Sunscreen. Even when clouds are prevalent, make sure to wear sunscreen as the sun intensity is strong.
    - Chapstick
    - Ibuprofen
    - Anti-diarrheal. None of us had any issues with food poisoning, but this should be standard for any trip
    - Gauze pads
    - Athletic tape
    - Various size bandages
    - Sewing scissors
    - Aquaphor or any petroleum jelly product
    - Earplugs

Food

There are inconclusive results regarding what food is allowed through customs in Peru. It seems to be pretty subjective, depending on the customs official on duty. Upon my arrival in Cusco, my sealed packaged meat products were confiscated. However, my companions had no issue bringing any of their similar meat products through customs in Lima. Products like packaged trail mix and freeze-dried backpacking meals were all acceptable. Typical trail foods like trail mix, granola bars, and oatmeal were hard to find in Huaraz but can be bought in Cusco at a premium price. There are stands in the San Pedro Market in Cusco where you can make your own trail mix with different nuts and dried fruits. It is a bit pricey, but you get to try some of the unusual dried fruits.

When you are not on the trail, Peru offers an incredibly rich array of cuisine. Lunch was the most important meal of the day for the locals. My favorite dining experiences were lunches at small local restaurants where you will not find a menu nor another tourist. Most places for lunch have a set menu with a few choices for an entrée. You can have a fantastic three-course meal with a drink for maybe $2. Food from all over the world can be found in Peru. Meat is abundant in the diets of Peruvian locals, but vegetarians can certainly navigate their way.

Smartphone Applications to Download

- Maps.me - This is an absolute must for any traveler. Maps.me provides offline map services with spectacular detail. Google Maps also allows you to download maps for offline usage, but Maps.me offers superior detail, especially for trekking. When you download the app, download different maps by zooming into the desired region. I was so impressed to find hiking trails shown on the maps and locations of gas stations, hostels, and restaurants wherever we traveled. Even without cellular data, the GPS in your phone tracks your location. Offline navigation with Maps.me puts getting lost in the past. I will be happy to share with you my GPS files for each trek that you can import into this app for offline viewing. Just email me at andyfineadventure@gmail.com with proof of book purchase.

- Yandex Translator – Excellent offline language translator application that does a pretty good job with most words and phrases. It is not perfect, but can frequently be a tool for communicating with locals.
- Tricount – This application helps keep track of costs for your trip and helps settle who owes what when someone pays for a shared expense.
- WhatsApp – Most of the locals communicate with WhatsApp, an internet-based communication service.
- TrackMyTour – Allows you to create an online map of your journey for family and friends to follow along. Parents love this as they can see in real-time what you are doing and that you are safe.
- MemoTrips – Essentially a digital travel journal, where you can document your journey with pictures and written entries.
- Hostelworld – Popular source to book hostels. Be aware that often prices are lower when you inquire directly to the hostel or campsite.
- Booking.com – Many lodging locations in Peru use Booking.com. A nice feature about this service is free cancellation on most reservations as long as you cancel within a couple of days of arrival.
- TripAdvisor – Get recommendations on activities, lodging, and restaurants in each destination.
- Airline App – Keeps track of your boarding passes and on certain flights, you can stream movies and tv shows directly to your device.

How to Use This Trekking Guide

The purpose of this trekking guide is to provide you with the necessary information for you to successfully plan and execute the trek. For each trek, I have provided self-designed trail maps with all of the essential information you need. Distance and moving times are listed for each segment of the map. The black and white dots mark the exact segment that these metrics are referring to. For every listed distance and time, find the black and white dots on the left and right, and that will indicate the associated segment. **The times that are listed are strictly moving time I required to complete the section. THEY ARE NOT TOTAL HIKING TIME.** The times listed do not include breaks, so factor this into your plan. Since everyone is going to require different frequency and duration of breaks, I sought to provide a more baseline metric that should apply to most trekkers. Figure most full days of hiking will require one to two hours of combined breaks, so make sure to factor that into your daily plan.

For each of the hikes, there are many different iterations of itineraries you can do. Some of the itineraries I will suggest might deviate from what I did based on hindsight. That is part of the joy of creating a guide. So that you can benefit and learn from my experience. Elevation profiles are included for each overall trek as well as individual days. Distance (miles) vs. Elevation (feet) are provided for more general topographical reference.

Eastern Peru: Salkantay, Machu Picchu and Ausangate

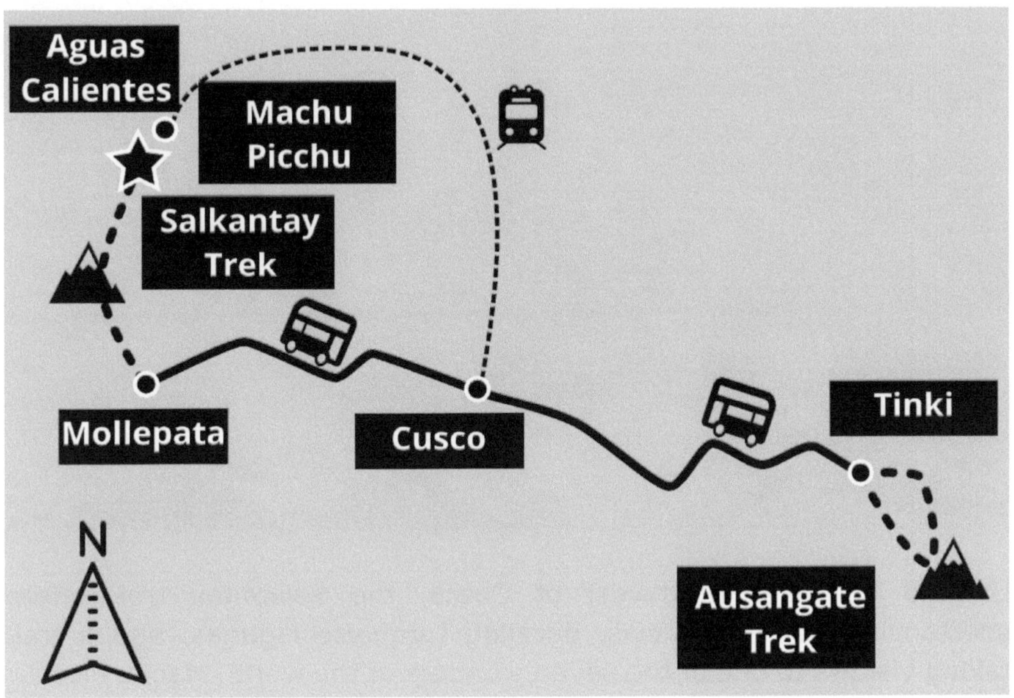

Salkantay Trek

Located 40 miles northwest of Cusco, the Salkantay trek offers spectacular mountain views, dazzling turquoise lagunas, and a trail taking visitors to one of the seven wonders of the world, Machu Picchu. Since the infamous Machu Picchu is the prize for completing this trek, it also comes with the largest crowds. It will take four to five days to complete this 55-mile hike. It is quite possible to do this trek without a guide. The availability of public transportation, lack of permit requirements, and easy-to-follow trails make this a great hike for moderate to advanced hikers to do independently. Even though this is the most trafficked trail in this guide, do not be fooled into thinking this is without a challenge. With the highest point reaching 15,279 ft, there is a severe amount of uphill and downhill to climb.

Several hiking trails lead to Machu Picchu, including the Inca, Choquequirao, Lares, and finally the Salkantay trek. The Inca trail is only an option if you are planning your trip far in advance and are willing to pay the hefty permit fees. We chose the Salkantay Trek because it reaches the highest altitude and is considered the most physically challenging of the routes with the best views. The other treks have the advantage of exploring more of the historical ruins. So, if that is more interesting to you than the high alpine peaks, perhaps consider those options instead.

Salkantay Trail Map

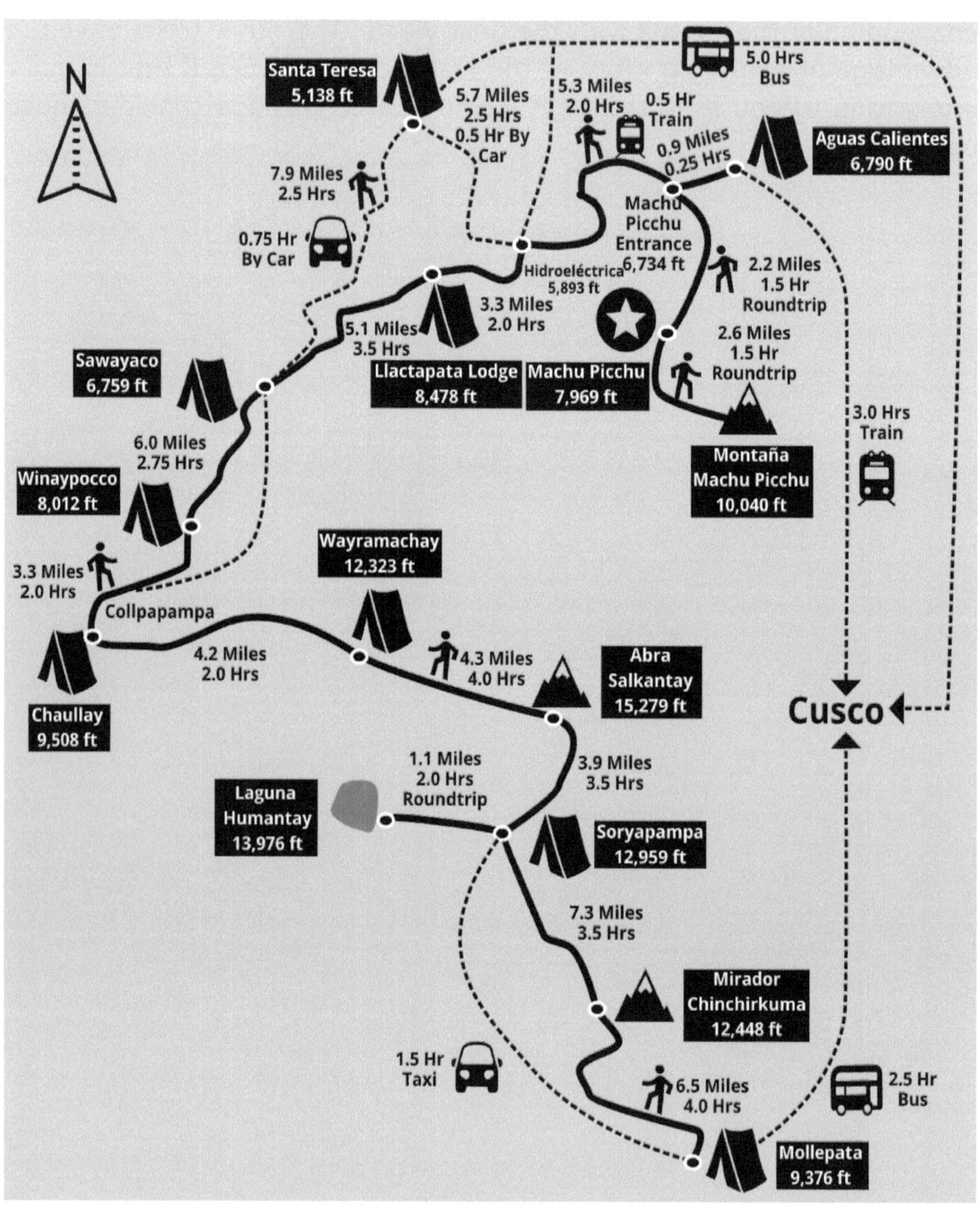

Logistics

The Salkantay trek starts at a town called Mollepata and ends at Machu Picchu outside of Aguas Calientes. To get to Mollepata, there is a bus stop in Cusco that takes 2.5 hours and costs 15 soles per person (~$4.50). Unfortunately, there is no marked bus terminal where you will find this bus. No signs will indicate that you are in the right spot. The bus stop looks like a driveway next to a couple of restaurants and the bus is more like a large passenger van than a coach. The stop is marked on Maps.me and has the following GPS coordinates: (-13.515732, -71.987641). It is not hard to find because as soon as you start walking on the block near it, there will be locals asking you if you are going to the Salkantay trek. Just ask any of these people where the bus to Mollepata is. The bus leaves approximately every hour starting very early but typically waits until it is full before departing. The drive to Mollepata is beautiful with a lot of elevation gain and loss as it leaves the valley.

Mollepata is a tiny village with a few convenience stores and some relatively expensive places to stay (around $50 per room). After stopping at a control point to pay the ten soles entrance fee, the bus drops you off in the main square of the town. You can start the trek from there, or you have the option to hire a taxi for about 80-100 soles to take you up to Soryapampa. The choice has its pros and cons both ways. The reason I recommend hiking this section of the trail is so you gradually gain the 3,600 feet of elevation throughout a day's hike instead of doing so quickly in a taxi ride. This will help mitigate altitude sickness risk. Plus, some really gorgeous points will be missed if you drive on the road up. On the other hand, I can see scenarios where taking the taxi would be the superior decision. The trail is pretty challenging with a lot of elevation gain, so it might be better for some to save their energy for the remaining parts of the hike that also offer more impressive views. Another advantage I can see to taking the taxi is getting to Laguna Humantay earlier in the day when the sun is higher and shining brightly on this glorious spot.

Costs

Item	Cost (Soles)
Bus to Mollepata	15 per person
Entrance Fee	10 per person
Mollepata Hotel	60 per person
Soryapampa Campsite	10 per tent
Wayramachay Campsite	10 per tent
Sawayaco Campsite	5 per tent
Aguas Calientes Hostel (2 Nights)	45 x 2=90 per person
Machu Picchu + Machu Picchu Mountain	200 per person
Taxi from Hidroeléctrica to Santa Teresa Hot Springs	15 per person
Private Ride for 3 people from Santa Teresa to Cusco	50 per person
TOTAL (excluding food)	**465 soles (~$140)**

Food and Water

All food will need to be packed in except for dinners in Chaullay, Llactapata Lodge, and Aguas Calientes where you can pay for dinner if you want a treat and to save the pack weight. You will find scattered stands along the route selling basic snacks and drinks, but do not rely on these. Water is plentiful and accessible throughout the entire trek. I never found it necessary to have more than two to three liters on my pack at a time.

Recommended Itinerary – 5 Day Salkantay

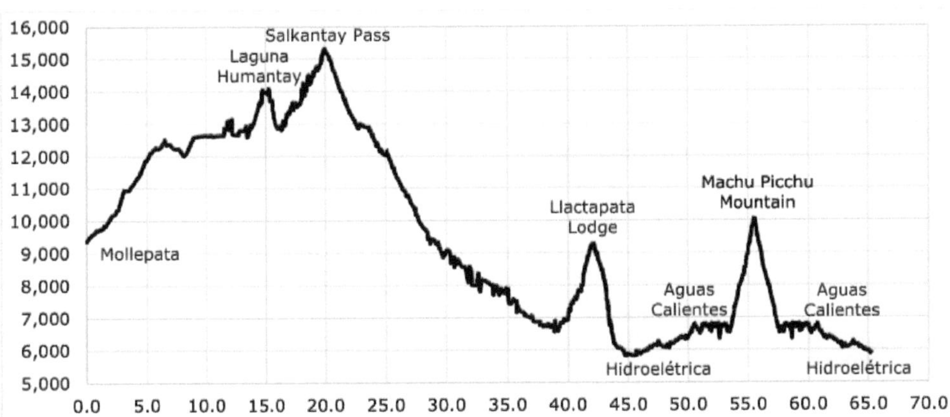

Day 0: Afternoon travel from Cusco to Mollepata. Stay in Mollepata.

There are two options for getting to Mollepata to start the trek. You can travel to Mollepata in the afternoon on Day 0 before you begin the trek and stay overnight, or you can take the first bus in between 04:00 and 05:00 on Day 1 to get you to Mollepata by about 07:30, early enough to start the trek. Waking up that early was not attractive to me, so we took an afternoon bus and stayed in a Mollepata hotel overnight.

Day 1: Mollepata to Soryapampa with Laguna Humantay

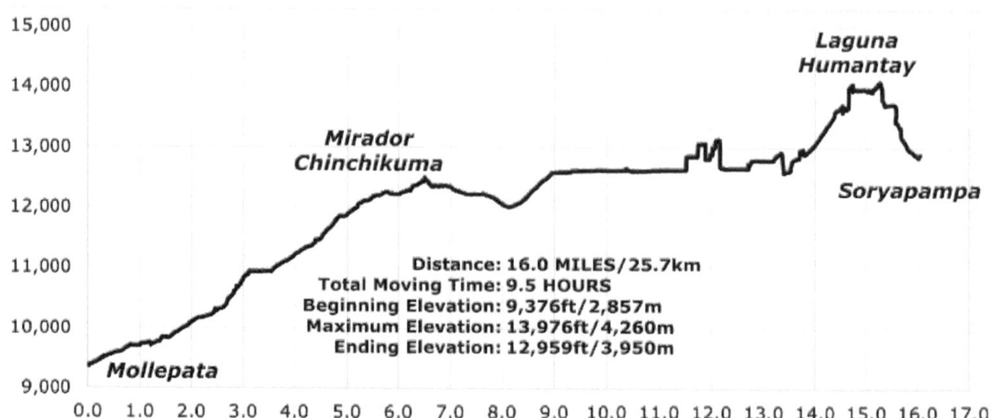

The hike from Mollepata to Soryapampa with a stop at Laguna Humantay is challenging with a lot of elevation gain. Starting from the village center in Mollepata, you will begin the first couple miles along the village road that climbs up to the mountains. Blue trail signs effectively show the way. Of all my hiking days in Peru, the section from Mollepata to the Mirador Chinchikuma was certainly the muddiest. It is clear that you are sharing a path with local horses and cows. By lunch, you will arrive at the Mirador Chinchikuma which reveals the first snowcapped peak of Mt. Tukarway.

Another 3.5 hours of hiking brings you to the village of Soryapampa. Set up camp in one of the paid shelters (10 soles per tent) before grabbing your day pack and heading up the trail to Laguna Humantay. It takes about an hour to climb the exhausting 1,000 feet up to the Laguna Humantay, but it is worth it. This gorgeous turquoise lake is a popular tourist destination since it can be visited as a day hike from Cusco. An advantage of arriving at the lake at the end of the day was avoiding these tourists. But getting there late did have the disadvantage of not having the sun shining on the lake. The lake was already so incredibly blue in the shade; I could only imagine how spectacular it must be with the sun shining.

Laguna Humantay: 13,976 feet

The descent back to Soryapampa will be a welcome change after a full day of uphill grinding. Enjoy a good night's sleep before Day 2 brings another day with serious uphill, with even better views than Day 1.

Day 2: Soryapampa to Chaullay via Salkantay Pass

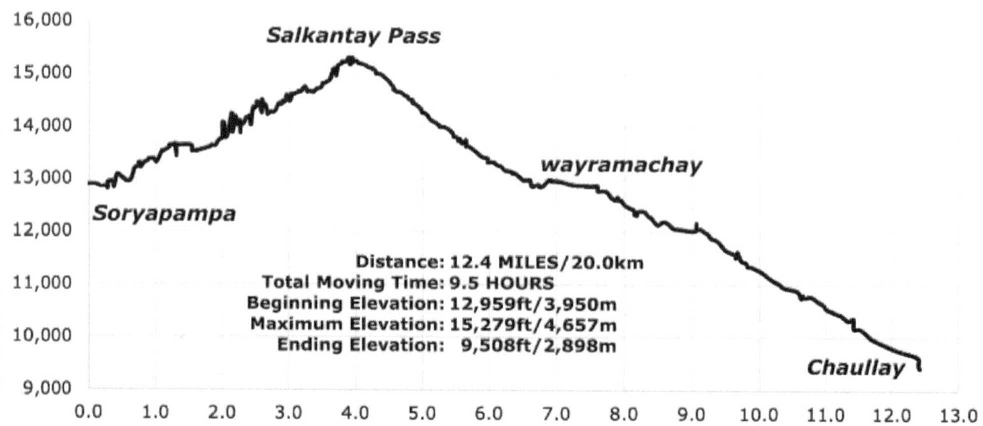

This is another challenging day with a lot of time on your feet and climbing up some severe elevation to reach one of the highlights of the trek, the Salkantay Pass. Start the day as early as possible. We did not reach Chaullay by the end of Day 2, only making it as far as Wayramachay. This is indeed what happened to us, but I recommend pushing this day harder than we did and make it to Chaullay. Most of the tour groups start this hike before the sun rises, and in hindsight, I recommend doing the same.

After sixty to ninety minutes of hiking, you will reach the tiny village of Salkantaypampa. Just past it yields an unmarked fork in the path. To the left leads to the challenging "seven snakes" path with a set of crazy steep switchbacks climbing a lot of elevation quickly. This is undoubtedly the more popular way to go. However, you can also consider the alternative path to the right. We could see a few of the guides taking the path to the right, and it appeared to be more gradual. After a nice break at the top of these switchbacks, there is still a significant final push up to the summit of the Salkantay Pass that will test your endurance and lower body strength.

Abra Salkantay: 15,279 feet

Staying too long admiring the Abra Salkantay was one factor that caused us not to make it to Chaullay on Day 2. Make sure to effectively pace out your time because after the pass there is still another six hours to get to Chaullay. The good news is that the trail is all downhill until you reach Chaullay. If you end up like us and only making it as far as Wayramachay on Day 2, you will be just fine. However, in order to make it to the beautiful Llactapacta Lodge by the end of the next day as I recommend, you need to make it to Chaullay on Day 2. In between the pass and Wayramachay is a small stand where you can buy some basic drinks and candy. Wayramachay is a beautiful place to camp with shelters to cook in and bathrooms you could pay to use. Chaullay offers more luxurious lodging options, a few places to eat, and even had a place where you can get a message.

Chaullay: 9,508 feet

Day 3: Chaullay to Llactapata Lodge

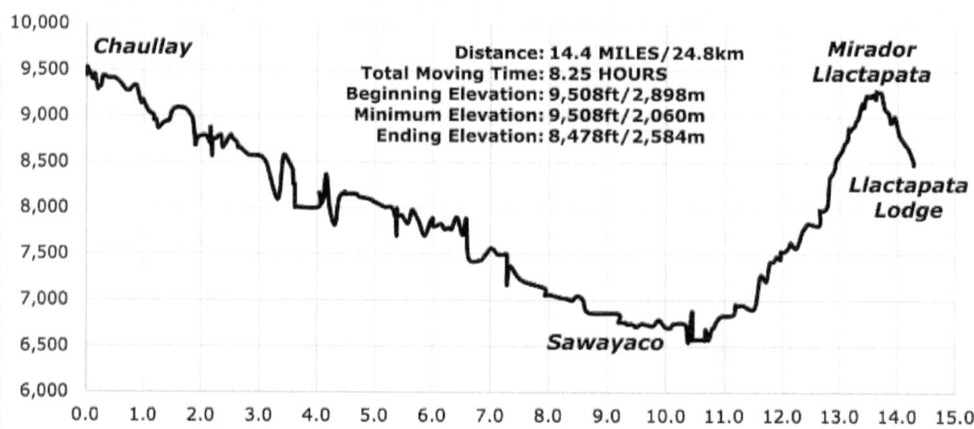

The scenery on Day 3 is strikingly different than Day 2. At this lower elevation, snowcapped peaks get exchanged for lush forest, and high alpine cold air gets traded for more tropical conditions. As my friend put it along the way, "There's so much life here!" From Chaullay, the trail follows the road to Collpapampa, then descends to the Rio Santa Teresa.

River Crossing past Collpapampa: (-13.316427, -72.667998)

There are two choices when you arrive at this river crossing just after Collpapampa. You can continue hiking along the road all the way to Sawayaco, or you can cross the river and hike on the nice forest trail that traces along the river. Depending on the time of year, mudslides can cause this section of the trail to close, forcing you to stay on the road. The road route will certainly be faster, but hiking on real dirt through some lovely forest is what I recommend. In between this river crossing and Sawayaco, you will find several small villages where you can buy basic drinks and snacks. Try to reach Sawayaco by lunchtime. Sawayaco is relatively pretty low in elevation at only 6,759 feet.

At Sawayaco, there is another fork giving you two different route options. The road heading northeast straight to Santa Teresa is one option, or you can take the more eastern route up to Llactapata Lodge. Going the Llactapata route is certainly tougher with 1,700 feet of elevation gain over 5.1 miles taking about 3-4 hours. But as typical with most trekking, the more strenuous route comes with superior views. I highly recommend the Llactapata route if you have the energy to do the climb. The peak at Llactapata Lodge offers beautiful views where you can see the Machu Picchu ruins in the distance while relaxing over a freshly cooked meal. From the end of Sawayaco, cross the river to the east side, then walk up the dirt road until you find a control station

(-13.213617, -72.617383) where an officer will ask for your passport and to fill out a logbook. From the control point, it is a steady uphill on a really nice forest trail lasting three to four hours until you reach Llactapata Lodge.

If you only make it to Sawayaco on Day 3, you can still take the Llactapata route on Day 4. It just means not getting to stay at the lodge without adding on another day to the trek.

Day 4: Llactapata Lodge to Aguas Calientes

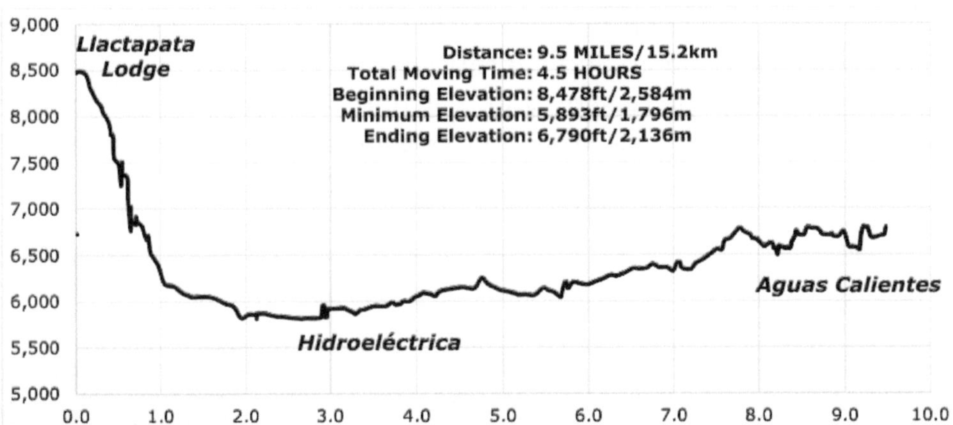

Day 4 is the last day of hiking before reaching Aguas Calientes, the gateway to Machu Picchu. After three strenuous days of hiking, Day 4 is the shortest and easiest of the trek with limited elevation gain. The hike begins with a steep descent through the jungle from Llactapata Lodge to Hidroeléctrica followed by a walk along the railroad that connects Hidroeléctrica to Aguas Calientes. From Hidroeléctrica there is an option to take the thirty-minute train to Aguas Calientes for 80 soles (~$25) each way. Or there is the scenic two to three-hour hike along the train tracks that weave along the Rio Urubamba to Aguas Calientes. Technically, walking along the tracks is not allowed, but everyone ignores this mandate.

Suspension Bridge in between Hidroeléctrica and Aguas Calientes

Once you arrive at Hidroeléctrica, you will be surrounded by all sorts of tourists traveling to Machu Picchu who clearly didn't reach the Salkantay Pass. The town of Aguas Calientes is a tourist town cluttered with restaurants, hostels, and overpriced souvenir markets. Save your souvenir shopping for Cusco; you will find the same stuff for lower prices. It is still fun to walk through the endless maze of vendor's stalls offering everything you can think of with a llama on it.

Aguas Calientes: 7,010 feet

Day 5: Aguas Calientes to Machu Picchu Mountain, Travel to Cusco via Hidroeléctrica or Stay in Aguas Calientes.

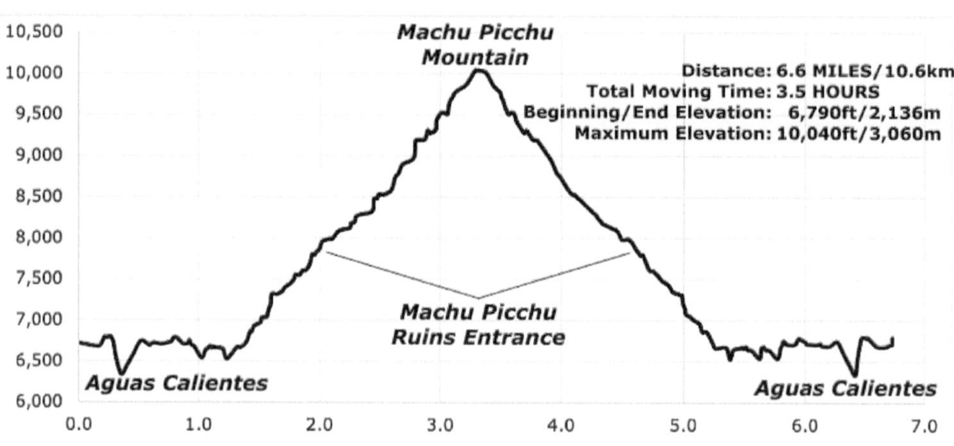

See the chapter on Machu Picchu for my complete guide to visiting Machu Picchu. Depending on what time slot you are granted to enter Machu Picchu, plan on leaving Aguas Calientes at least an hour before to reach Machu Picchu. To start the hike up to Machu Picchu, find the control station fifteen minutes outside of Aguas Calientes (-13.161244, -72.52616). From the control station, you'll hike 45-60 minutes up to the Machu Picchu entrance. We bought tickets both to enter the ruins as well as to climb to the summit of Machu Picchu mountain. It takes an hour to hike up to the summit from the central area of the ruins.

Machu Picchu Mountain: 10,040 feet

Once you've sufficiently taken in this wonder of the world, descend back down to Aguas Calientes either by hiking down the same trail or taking the bus. If you have time to extend your trip by a day, stay in Aguas Calientes for another night to avoid rushing your visit to this all-time bucket list destination. But if you need to get to Cusco in a hurry, you certainly would have time to get back either by taking the train out of Cusco or the bus out of Hidroeléctrica the same day.

Optional Day 6: Travel to Santa Teresa's Hot Springs Before Returning to Cusco.

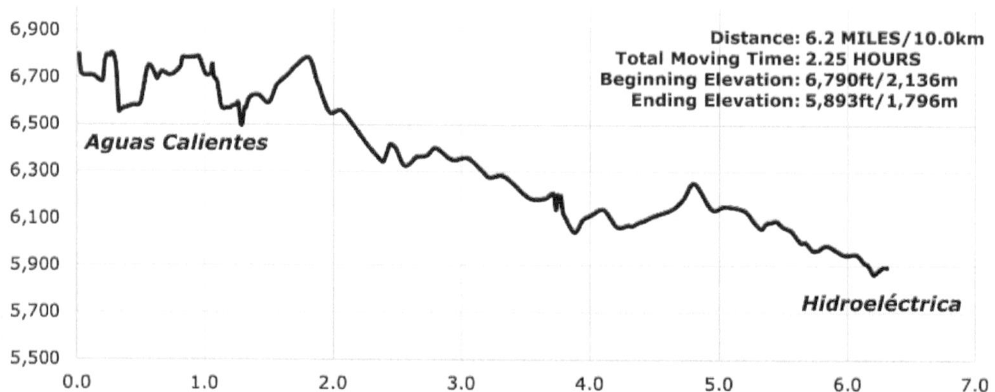

If you have time to extend the Salkantay Trek by a day, I highly recommend a stop in nearby Santa Teresa for a soak in the natural hot springs. Leave Aguas Calientes for Hidroeléctrica where you can hire a taxi to take you to the Santa Teresa hot springs for 40 soles. These delightful hot springs provide some needed muscle relaxation after completing a demanding hike.

Santa Teresa Hot Springs (-13.109701, -72.600758)

Route Alternatives

- If you are stretched for time, you could reduce the trek by hiring a ride from Sawayaco to Hidroeléctrica then either walk or take the train to Aguas Calientes.
- Going through Santa Teresa instead of Llactapata is easier and faster. You could fit in a stop to the hot springs on Day 3.

Machu Picchu

Tickets for Machu Picchu

To reduce the congestion on this UNESCO World Heritage site, the number of daily visitors is limited. Reservations are required to enter the ruins. Purchase your tickets on the Official Machu Picchu Tickets Website (https://www.machupicchu.gob.pe/inicio) before your trip. There are three different ticket options available:

- Machu Picchu Only: Provides access to the general Machu Picchu ruins. Here is where all of the classic Machu Picchu pictures are taken. If you do not want to hike up to either Waynapicchu or Machu Picchu Mountain, this is the only ticket you need. You can typically get these tickets the night before at the ticket office in Aguas Calientes. Cost: 152 soles (~$46).
- Machupicchu con montana Waynapicchu: This ticket includes entrance to the general Machu Picchu ruins plus the option to hike to the summit of Waynapicchu. Waynapicchu is the tall

mountain that you see in the backdrop past the ruins in the classic pictures of Machu Picchu. It is a shorter hike than Machu Picchu mountain with a great view of the ruins. These tickets typically sell out 2-3 months in advance. Cost: 200 soles (~$60).

- Machupicchu con montana Machupicchu: Similar to the Waynapicchu ticket, this option will grant you access both to the general Machu Picchu ruins and Machu Picchu Mountain. The Machu Picchu Mountain takes 60-90 minutes to climb up the over 2,000 feet of elevation gain. It is a challenging hike to the top, but the views of the ruins from the top are spectacular and well worth it. Cost: 200 soles (~$60).

All tickets have a defined time window associated with them. This time specifies the earliest time that you can enter the site. The most popular option is the earliest entrance at 06:00. If you can secure these tickets, definitely do it because you get to have a whole hour where you practically have the ruins to yourself before the masses join the party. There might be more clouds in the early morning, but the serenity of walking the grounds is extraordinary. You can always enter the ruins after the time assigned to your ticket. Visitors can stay in the grounds for as long as the ruins are open.

You need to have your tickets printed before entering the ruins. We were lucky that our hostel host informed us of this when we arrived in Aguas Calientes. If you do not have your tickets printed, you can get them printed for free at the ticket office in Aguas Calientes (-13.154184, -72.525316). Just make sure you have your email confirmation available on your phone.

Getting to Machu Picchu

The first step in getting to Machu Picchu is traveling to Aguas Calientes. If you are doing the Salkantay Trek or other alternatives such as the Lares, Inca, and Choquequirao, this is built into that itinerary. Those wishing to get to Machu Picchu directly from Cusco have several options:

- Luxury train directly from Cusco's Poroy station to Aguas Calientes via Peru Rail. This is the easiest way to get to the ruins where you can sip wine and watch the gorgeous countryside. If you have limited time and are looking for the physically simplest option, this would be best. Prices fluctuate throughout the season but figure it is around $200 round trip per person.
- Ground transportation offered by many tour companies in Cusco will take you to Hidroeléctrica and back for around $20 and take 5-6 hours. To get from Hidroeléctrica to Aguas Calientes, you can either hike the two to three hours along the train tracks or take the $25 train.

Aguas Calientes is the gateway to the entrance of Machu Picchu, but it isn't exactly where you will find the ruins. Aguas Calientes rests 900 feet below the Machu Picchu ruins. To get to Machu Picchu requires either a thirty-minute bus ride ($24 Roundtrip) or 45-60 minute hike up. Tickets for the bus can be bought in Aguas Calientes the night before. The queues for these buses can be extreme. Be prepared to wait at least an hour for the bus going both up and down. If you don't mind walking down, it might be a better idea for you to buy a one-way ticket up to the ruins and then walk down to avoid the enormous lines waiting to return to Aguas Calientes.

Those looking to hike up to Machu Picchu have to start at the control point before climbing up to the ruins. They do not begin processing hikers through this point until 05:00. At a swift pace, the earliest you will get to the entrance if you hike, will be at 05:45. Unfortunately, this is likely going to be after the first bus arrives from Aguas Calientes. If it is important for you to be the first in line at the ruins, you'll have to take the first bus up.

More Machu Picchu Tips

- I highly recommend hiring a pickup guide at the main entrance to Machu Picchu. Without understanding the history, Machu Picchu is just a pretty sight. A guide will help turn this opportunity from simply an Instagram picture into a rich learning experience that will provide a much deeper appreciation for the site. Guides can be hired at the entrance from about $15 to $30 per person depending on the group size. Experience, training, and price will fluctuate from guide to guide. There is an official rule that every visitor is required to have a guide. This is not enforced whatsoever. You can enter the ruins without a guide if that is your preference.
- The only bathrooms available are outside the entrance of Machu Picchu for a small fee. You will not find any bathrooms inside the ruins.
- Bring your own water! There are surprisingly no shops inside the ruins and minimal options outside of the entrance. You are allowed to bring your own food inside, but only eat in the designated areas.
- When you leave the gates of the ruins, don't forget to get your passport stamped! There is a small spot easily missed outside the exit where you can stamp your passport with an official Machu Picchu stamp.

Ausangate Trek

Towering to almost 21,000 feet, Mt. Ausangate is Peru's fifth highest peak and home to one of the best treks found in this region. Inspiring mountain views, surreal turquoise lakes, and breathtaking landscapes make this a hiker's treasure. While the Salkantay Trek attracts masses of tourists looking to visit Machu Picchu, the Ausangate Trek (pronounced "aus-an-got-tay") attracts hikers looking for more solitude without sacrificing scenery. Located three hours southeast of Cusco, the Ausangate Trek also offers experienced hikers the option of visiting the seemingly man-made Rainbow Mountain. The trek can be completed independently by any experienced hiker that has appropriately acclimatized to the high altitude. Unlike the Salkantay, the Ausangate Trek is consistently at high elevations at least 14,000 feet with its highest point at 16,766 feet (5,110 meters).

There are many different iterations possible to complete this trek. The classic Ausangate Trek is simply the path circumnavigating 41 miles around the mountain taking as little as four days. Visitors with ample time can extend this basic path to seven nights and 52 miles to include more segments of this incredible paradise. Similar to other Peruvian treks, mileage is not the best characteristic metric when gauging the difficulty of the trek. Certain days only put 6.5 miles under your feet but come with 3,200 feet of net elevation gain. Navigation can be challenging within individual sections of the Ausangate. Trails seem to evaporate below your feet, and you will be faced with a labyrinth of trails that could either be an actual footpath, or more likely one of the hundreds of paths forged by the grazers that populate this area.

If you are forced to choose between the Salkantay Trek and the Ausangate Trek, it mostly comes down to how important it is to see Machu Picchu. Reaching the wonder of the world might be one of your main incentives to travel to Peru in the first place. Between the choice of completing Salkantay/Machu Picchu and Ausangate, I recommend the Salkantay because Machu Picchu is truly spectacular and required for any visit to Peru. However, the scenery and quality of the hike at the Ausangate Trek are superior to the Salkantay Trek. Also, solitude seekers will find far fewer visitors sharing the trail. The Ausangate is more arduous with more significant elevation gains and more complicated logistics. If quality trekking is your priority for this adventure and you are equipped for the challenge, the Ausangate is the grander choice.

Logistics

The Ausangate Trek is a loop that starts and ends at the small town of Tinki, about three hours southeast of Cusco. To get to Tinki from Cusco, you can hire a private vehicle for about 100 soles (~$38), or there is a public bus that costs 10 soles per person (~$3.3). For a three to four-hour bus ride, the price is unbeatable. Similar to heading to the Salkantay, there is not an official bus terminal where you will find the bus going to Tinki. The bus that you are looking for is going to a town called Ocongate. Look for a bus with a sign for Ocongate (-13.527045, -71.958118). Buses leave sporadically throughout the day. I recommend showing up early and waiting until the bus appears. There is no timetable that I have been able to verify. It is a much more comfortable ride compared to the bus that takes you to Mollepata.

It is most popular to hike the Ausangate counterclockwise; however, clockwise is a suitable alternative to consider. My recommendation is to go counterclockwise because the views are better paced in increasing quality in this direction. Also, I recommend counterclockwise so that your stop at the Pacchanta hot springs is at the conclusion of your hike instead of the beginning. Once you arrive in Tinki, there are dirt roads that connect to Upis and Pacchanta. You have the option to hire transportation to take you to either of these spots from the main village square. We elected to hike up to Upis, and then pay for a motorbike ride to take us from Pacchanta back to Tinki after the trek. This turned out to be a wise decision and well worth the 30 soles per person price to save our knees from k1,800 feet of elevation descent.

All food and gear for the trip should be packed before departing Cusco. Tinki does not have anything resembling a supermarket. There were a few places to buy some basic items like pasta and canned vegetables. It was difficult to find even a restaurant to serve breakfast when we arrived. No reservations or advanced permits are required for the Ausangate Trek. You will pay an entrance fee ticket and minor campsite fees with cash along the way.

Costs

Item	Cost (Soles)
Transportation to Tinki	10 per person
Ausangate Entrance Fee	10 per person
Upis Campground	5 per tent

Anatapata Campground	20 per tent
Rainbow Mountain Pass	10 per person
Ausangate Lake Campground	10 per person
Jampa Campground	10 per person
Panchatta Hot Springs	5 per person
Motorbike from Panchatta to Tinki	30 per person
Tinki to Cusco Bus	10 per person
Total (not including food)	**115 soles (~$35)**

Ausangate Trail Map

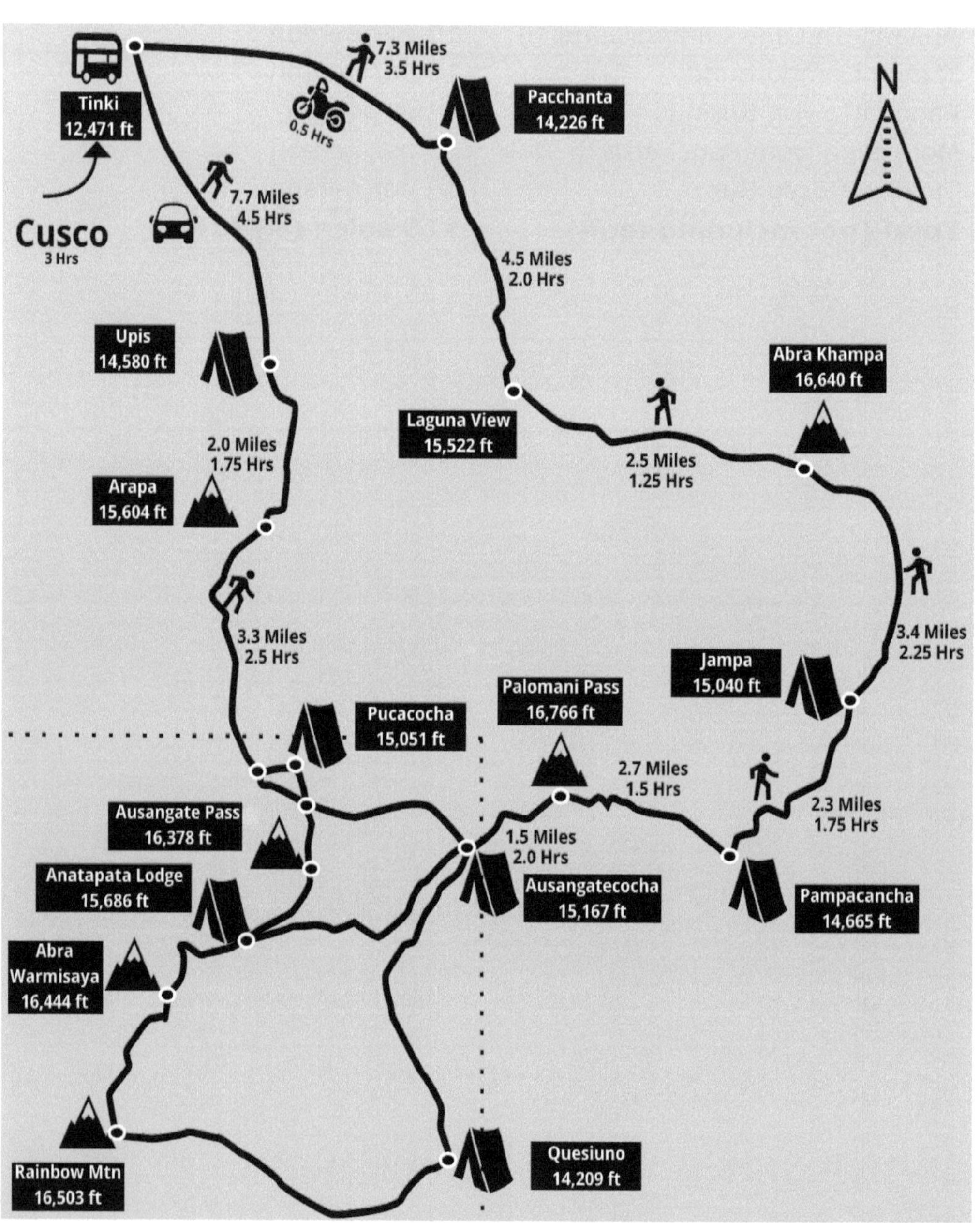

Ausangate Quadrant

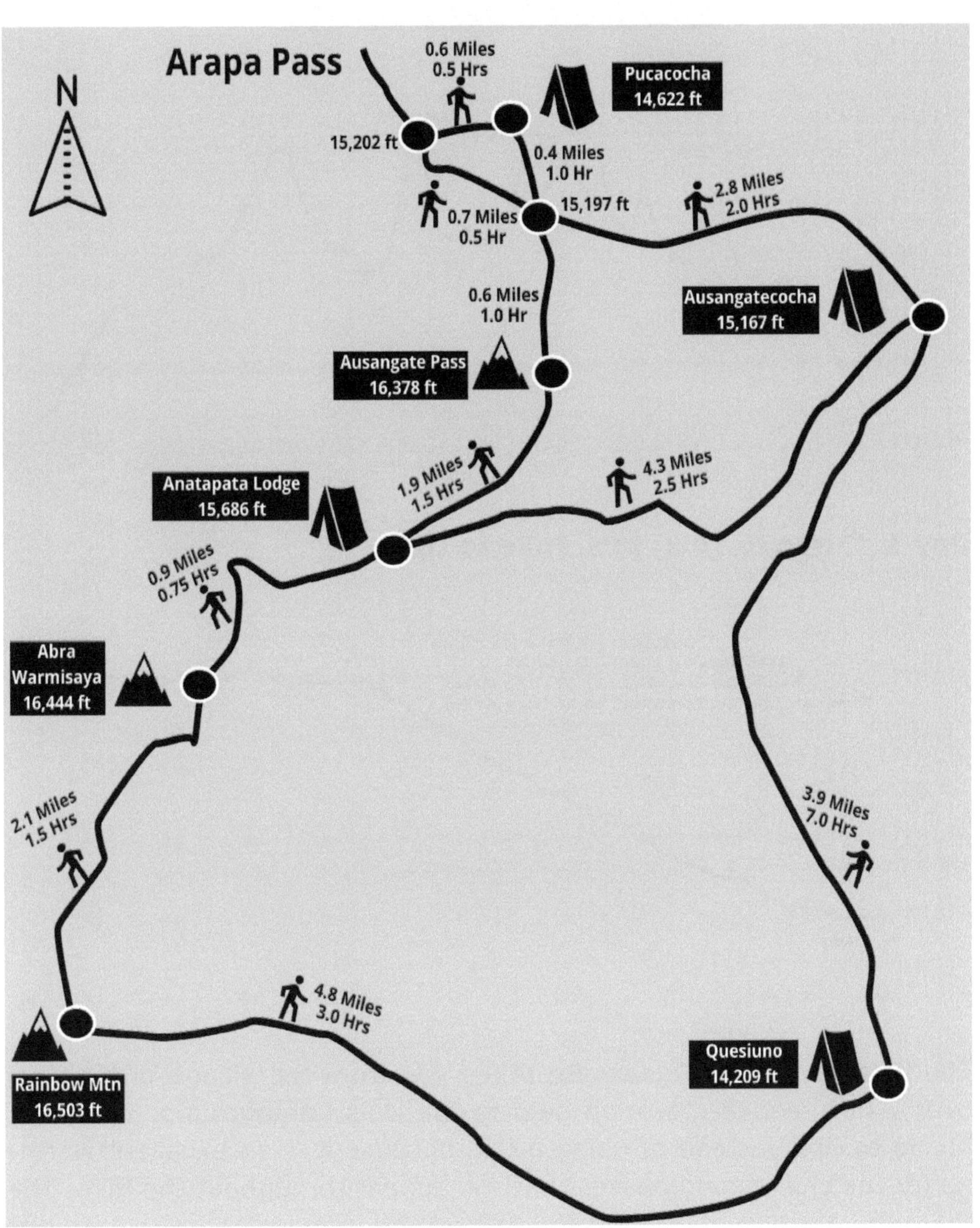

Recommended Itinerary - 5 Night Ausangate with Rainbow Mountain

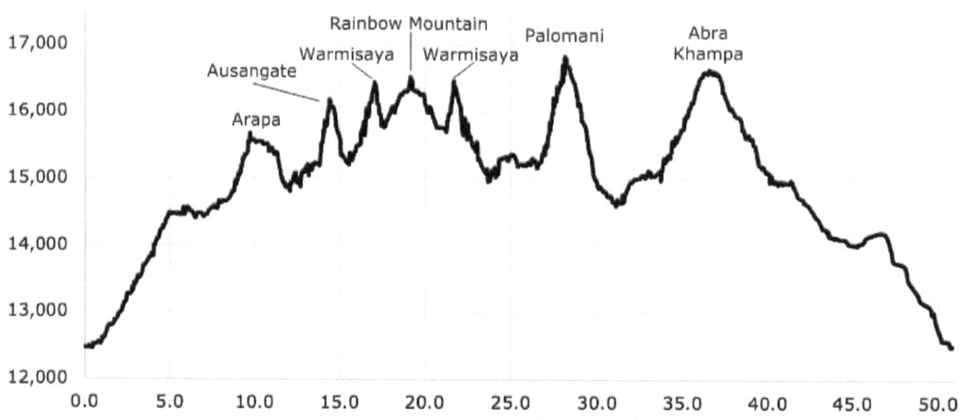

Day 1: Cusco to Tinki Bus. Hike to Upis.

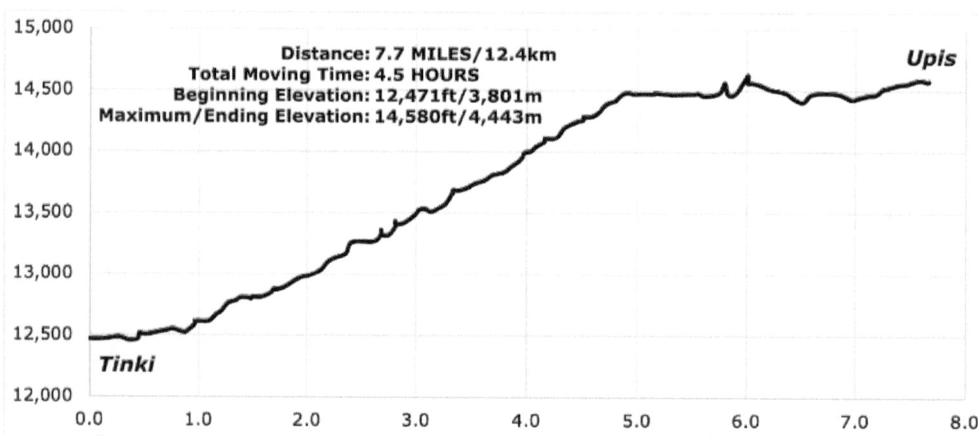

The first day of the Ausangate takes you from the village of Tinki up over 2,000 feet of elevation gain to the Upis Campground. I suggest hiking to Upis instead of using a taxi because it is an excellent warm-up for the challenging passes that will appear throughout the hike. The

Upis Campground is essentially the trailhead to the actual trek. The land that spans Tinki to Upis is comprised of dirt roads running through expansive agricultural land owned by the locals. You will see a plethora of cows, alpacas, and all sorts of other animals grazing over this paradise with Mt. Ausangate in the background.

Once you arrive in Tinki from Cusco in the morning, you will find the start of the hike by following the small road just east of the main village center. This road turns into a dirt road that travels up towards the towering Ausangate. It gets confusing towards the middle of the day because there are a lot of networking dirt roads, but as long as you continue hiking uphill towards Ausangate, you will find Upis. The last third or so of the hike to Upis will be off of the dirt roads and force you to hike through vast open fields that are difficult to navigate. It is a challenging ascent up to the campground and took us 4.5 hours of hiking time to complete. At Upis, the owner offered a hot spring for us to use high on the hill. We were exhausted from the day, so we chose not to investigate it. The campground offers fantastic views of Ausangate with water and toilet facilities.

Upis Campground: 14,580 feet

Day 2: Upis to Anatapata Lodge via Arapa and Ausangate Pass

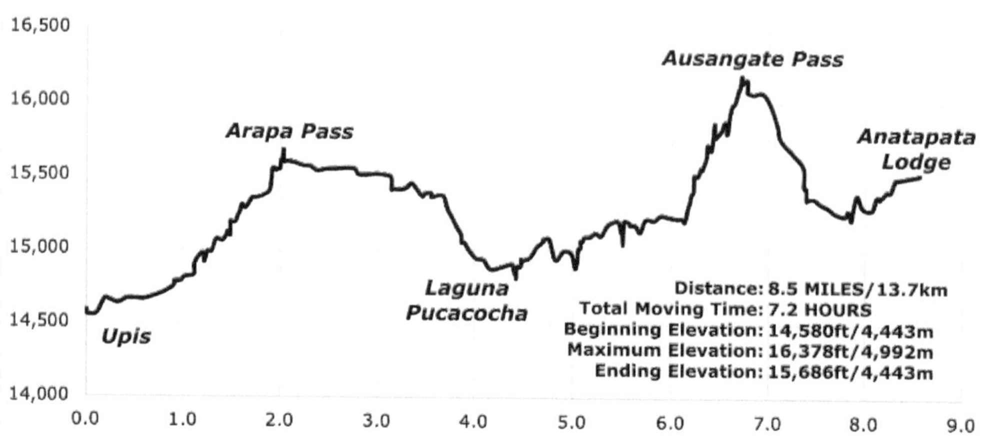

Day 2 of the Ausangate contains two sections that can either be split into two relatively short days or combined into one challenging day. We elected to complete both segments in one day due to time restrictions. It turned out to be a jam-packed day of hiking to complete both of these segments. The full day is only 8.5 miles, but again, mileage is not the best metric for measuring hiking difficulty here. High altitude, confusing navigation, and significant elevation gain over short distances make this a leg-scorcher of a day. There are two passes to be conquered. The first pass starts immediately upon your departure from the Upis Campground and climbs 1,100 feet up to the Arapa Pass. The trail up to the Arapa Pass is straightforward to follow and takes under two hours. The top is a beautiful spot where we enjoyed a snack break before continuing down towards Laguna Pucacocha. As you descend, you'll likely encounter different herds of alpacas and some smaller turquoise lakes. There is an excellent viewpoint that would make for a fantastic lunch spot (-13.806800, -71.280833).

As you approach Laguna Pucacocha in the early afternoon, there will be an unmarked point in the trail where you can descend off of the high ridge and downhill towards the large lake. There is a campground located on the southeastern corner of the lake. However, if you do not want to stop early at this campground, stay high on the path. If you continue east on this path, it will eventually lead to the Ausangatecocha Campground. Navigating to the Ausangate Pass was difficult. To get to the Ausangate Pass, you need to head south up the incredibly steep face with Laguna Pucacocha at your back. We were unable to find a trail that diverted uphill south to where we knew the pass was located. There were certainly no trail signs indicating when you should begin this ascent. I cannot offer better guidance for this section other than to forge your path uphill until you find a trail. My GPS path will undoubtedly work, but it may not be the most optimal. Towards the top, I was able to find a trail, so it is unclear if we should have cut uphill to the south earlier than we did or if there isn't a trail until you start getting higher up. It is an exceptionally steep climb up to the Ausangate Pass, taking a strenuous hour from the main trail diversion.

After the summit of the Ausangate, the navigating gets a lot easier all the way to Anatapata Lodge. You'll descend and veer to the west, then follow the valley uphill until you reach Anatapata Lodge. The Anatapata Lodge is a large cabin towards the end of the valley offering a comfortable stay for paying customers on a tour. It was unclear where we were supposed to set up our tents because the workers said we could not set up our tents anywhere in front of the property. We found a site where we could set up our tents further up the valley from the lodge and on the north side of the ridge. Just hike past the lodge and turn right after a few minutes, scrambling uphill until you find the nice flat section worthy of your tent for the night.

Day 3: Anatapata Lodge -> Abra Warmisaya -> Rainbow Mountain -> Ausangatecocha

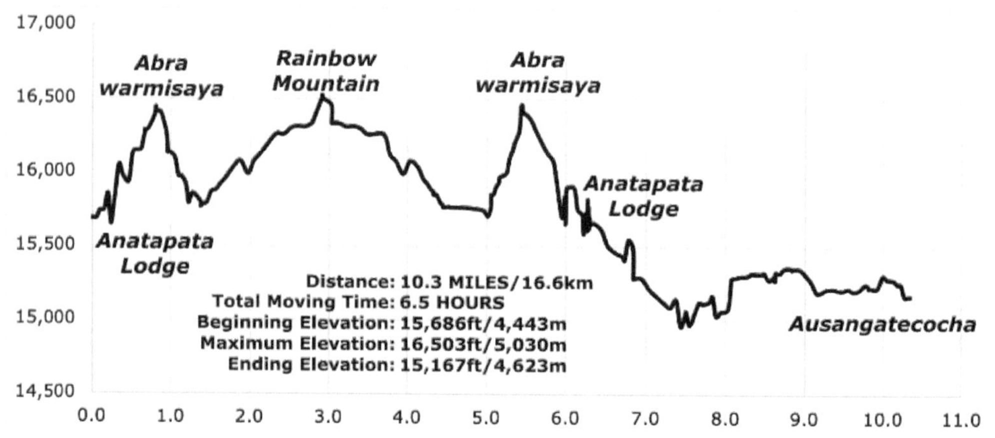

Day 3 of the Ausangate Trek is highlighted by the seemingly man-made Rainbow Mountain. When you look at this unbelievable gem, you truly are looking at millions of years of geological history. This geological wonder is the result of sedimentary layers' unique mineralogy and effects from weathering. Iron oxide rust gives the vibrant red coloration seen in mountains all around this range. The Rainbow Mountain has become one of the most significant tourist attractions in the area bringing hundreds of visitors a day from Cusco to capture this Instagram-worthy picture. Anyone can complete this day trip. Only you will have truly earned the view by completing a full multi-day trek to see it.

Since we would be returning to Anatapata at midday, we only needed daypacks for the trip to Rainbow Mountain. There is a woman named Margarita who owns a cabin just uphill of the Anatapata Lodge who offered to store our bags for 20 soles. To me, this was less risky than leaving all of our gear unattended for the morning. To avoid the buzzing crowds of tourists that infiltrate the Rainbow Mountain, we began the hike from Anatapata Lodge early at 05:30. I loved hiking during the stillness of dawn and watching the sunrise. It takes less than an hour to ascend the 750 feet up to the summit of Abra Warmisaya at 16,444 feet. Watching the sunrise from this epic viewpoint was an incredible highlight. You then quickly descend the steep southern face and lose almost all of the elevation that you gained. When you get to the bottom of the valley, you'll find a small lake (-13.85181, -71.29331). There is no clear path from this unnamed lake uphill to the Rainbow Mountain. From this south end of the lake, head directly west and then curve south uphill. Once you find the trail after the lake, it is pretty easy to follow all the way up. It took us about 2.5 hours total to hike from the Anatapata Lodge to the top of the viewpoint for Rainbow Mountain, arriving right around 08:00. As you approach the viewpoint, you'll be asked to pay a ten soles entrance fee. We were barely beaten to the viewpoint by the first bus of motivated tourists who took the earliest tour from Cusco. From 08:00-09:00 there weren't too many tourists, but by 09:30 the crowds started to creep up on us. In hindsight, I would have left camp by 05:00 to beat the crowds and have some tranquility with the mountain without the buzz of tourists. It would have made the incredible site more authentic and wilder than when the crowds create a more commercialized experience.

From the Rainbow Mountain, we returned to the Anatapata Lodge via Abra Warmisaya before continuing to Ausangatecocha. Another option you could consider is to continue east from Rainbow Mountain past the tourist bus parking lot and through the valley to the Quesiuno Campground. Then the following day, there is a valley north that takes you to Ausangatecocha. The path from Anatapata Lodge down to Ausangatecocha was the most challenging segment to navigate throughout the entire trek. These were the only hours of hiking that I honestly wished to have had a guide showing us the way. If you study my GPS path, you will see my staggering zig-zag path trying to navigate over a roller coaster of hills and around property boundaries made by local farmers. It was challenging to discern what was a real hiking path and what were animal grazing paths. As you continue east along the valley, stay high on the north ridge. Do not descend all the way to the valley floor as I initially did. You will see a deep red mountain ahead on your left side. Once you pass this red peak, the path leading northeast to Ausangatecocha becomes well defined and easy to follow. Depending on how well you navigate this portion, it could vary from two to three hours of hiking to get to Ausangatecocha from Anatapata Lodge. Even though it was difficult to navigate, I still recommend this route because it offered great views and saves you a whole day compared to going the long route through Camp Quesiuno. The campground at Ausangatecocha is just south of the lake. Make sure to hike up to the lake for some gorgeous views before grabbing some shut eye in preparation for the best day of the entire trek.

Day 4: Ausangatecocha to Jampa Campground via Palomani Pass

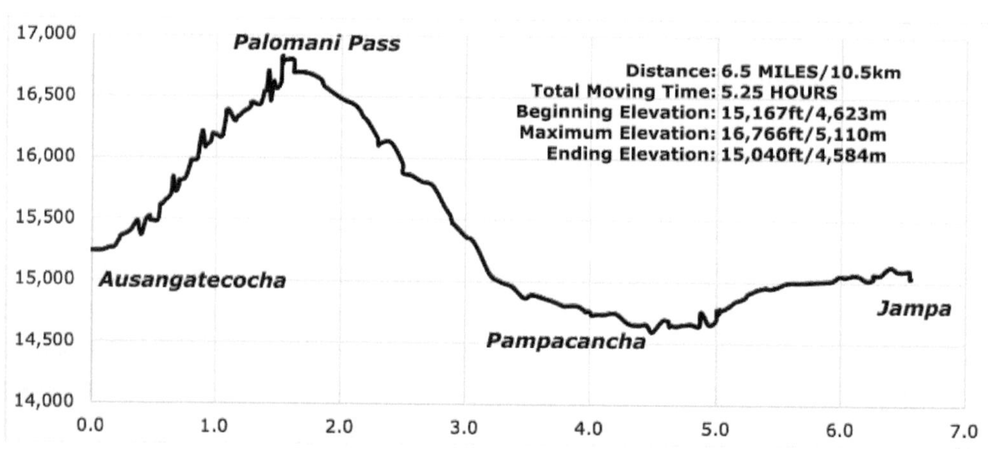

The fourth day of the Ausangate Trek is magical. It is a challenging day with two significant climbs and some perplexing navigation. However, the views granted to those who can make the climb rival anything on Planet Earth. The hike begins immediately with a two-hour, 1,600 ft climb up to the summit of the Palomani Pass. Navigation up to the pass is effortless, but your legs will start to scold you for not doing more of the stair stepper. It took our group two hours of hiking time, about 2.5 hours total to reach the top. The views from the pass are stunning. You'll see both Ausangatecocha and Pucacocha lakes as well as the Ausangate Pass from Day 2. You can afford a generous break to catch your breath, enjoy a snack, and soak in the fantastic views before descending the other side of the pass.

Incredible scenery east of Palomani Pass

The fantastic hiking of Day 4 only gets better after the Palomani Pass. As you descend 2,100 feet towards Pampacancha, the views of Mt. Ausangate are stunning. The glacier off the southeastern face stretches for miles as you hike along the back face of the Palomani Pass. You may find tour groups stopped at the Pampacancha Campground, but you should have time to continue to the far superior Jampa Campground. As you head northeast from Pampacancha, stay low and hug the left side of the valley until you find a wide-open marsh with steep cascades of rock and a waterfall on your left. Once you cross the marsh, you will find a trail that quickly gains elevation until it reaches Jampa Campground. I adored the hike from the Palomani Pass to Jampa

Campground because of the highly dynamic scenery as you curve around the mountain. You will be amazed by one view, see it disappear, and realize that there is an entirely new mountain face that revealed itself. The stretch after Pampacancha was another navigationally difficult section with zero trail signs, but we were able to find our destination with plenty of time to spare. The Jampa Campground was a stunning place to set up a tent and even had a tiny shop where you could purchase some basic food items.

Jampa Campground: 15,040 feet

Day 5: Jampa Campground to Pacchanta via Abra Khampa

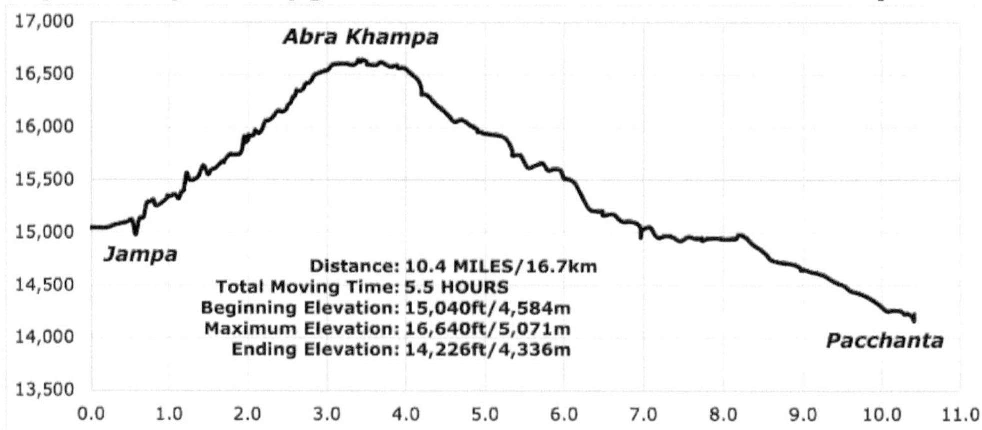

Day 5 will take you up to the phenomenal Khampa Pass, past a series of gorgeous turquoise lakes, and ending at the village of Pacchanta where you can enjoy a nice cooked meal and soak in the soothing natural hot springs. The day starts off with another challenging morning climb 1,500 feet up to the top to the Khampa Pass. It is a beautiful trail leading up to the pass with straightforward navigation, even though you'll have trouble spotting the actual pass much before you arrive. At the summit are breathtaking views of the neighboring Pacchanta Mountain whose jagged features reminded me much of the Salkantay Pass. We enjoyed our last lunch of the trek at this picturesque oasis before descending the western side of the pass.

Khampa Pass: 16,640 feet

Less than an hour of descent from the pass will lead you to a fork in the trail (-13.76289, -71.19822). As instructed by a local guide, we veered left at the fork and followed the signs towards Camp Gratis. This was a moment where I reflected on the importance of asking fellow guides and trekkers for advice even if I felt that I knew the way. My prior research didn't instruct me what to do at this junction. We were so lucky to learn that the far superior route is to go left because of the impeccable lake views you get along the way. Once you pass the Laguna Mirador (-13.76383, -71.21236), the trail steeply descends to the valley floor. You'll hike past one of the guide company campgrounds along a trail that is easy to follow. For those that seek the thrill of a rock jump into crystal clear but freezing glacial water, there is an excellent one on this segment of the trail in between the Laguna Mirador and Pacchanta (-13.75876, -71.22538). The final push to Pacchanta takes you along rivers and rolling hills but none requiring you to take out your Maps.me too often.

Upon arriving in Pacchanta, we struggled to find the camping spot indicated on Maps.me. It was getting late, so we accepted an offer from a local to set up camp in their backyard for an extremely fair price. We then walked into town to the only restaurant we could find and had some delicious pasta for dinner. After a well-earned hearty dinner, we joined some other trekkers and locals for a night soak in the hot springs right in the city center. Watching the stars come out by the millions as we let our muscles relax in hot water was an incredible way to finish the trek.

Day 6: Pacchanta to Tinki. Bus to Cusco.

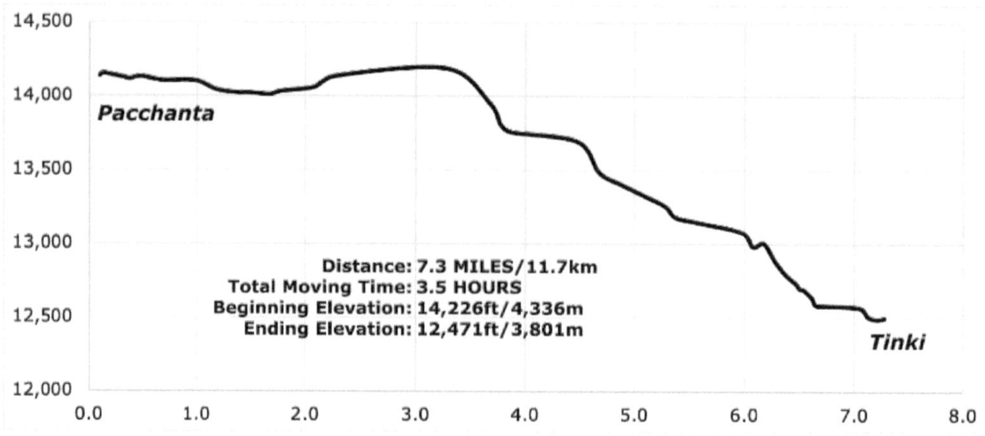

On Day 6, we decided to save the beating on our legs and take a thirty-minute motorbike ride back down to Tinki instead of enduring the 7.3 miles with 1,800 feet of elevation descent without any impressive views. The ride was absolutely worth the 30 soles per person to eliminate the impact on my knees from such long descent. You only need to ask around the village, and there will be someone with a bike you can negotiate with for a ride down to Tinki. After arriving in Tinki, you can ride back to Cusco on the same bus that brought you to Tinki. Wait on the north side of the street by the village square for the bus to arrive (-13.66677, -71.32101). It took a long four hours to return to Cusco since the bus waited almost an hour to pick up more passengers in Oconogate. However, for ten soles per person, you cannot complain.

Alternative Ausangate Itinerary

The Ausangate Trek could be completed in as little as four days for the time constrained trekker. For those in a time pinch, it will require eliminating the Rainbow Mountain excursion. However, the hike circumventing Mt. Ausangate is still a fabulous hike. Here is a summary of the itinerary I suggest if you are pressed for time but still want to fit Ausangate in your schedule.

Day 1: Take the early morning bus from Cusco to Tinki. Hire a taxi from Upis to Tinki. Hike from Upis through the Arapa Pass to Pucacocha.
Day 2: Pucacocha to Jampa. It is a full and challenging day, but rushed trekkers should be able to hike to Ausangatecocha from Pucacocha, over the Palomani Pass, and make it to Jampa in one day.
Day 3: Jampa to Pacchanta. Same as Day 5 in recommended itinerary.
Day 4: Pacchanta to Tinki (motorbike or hike). Bus back to Cusco.

Northern Peru: Cordilleras Blanca and Huayhuash

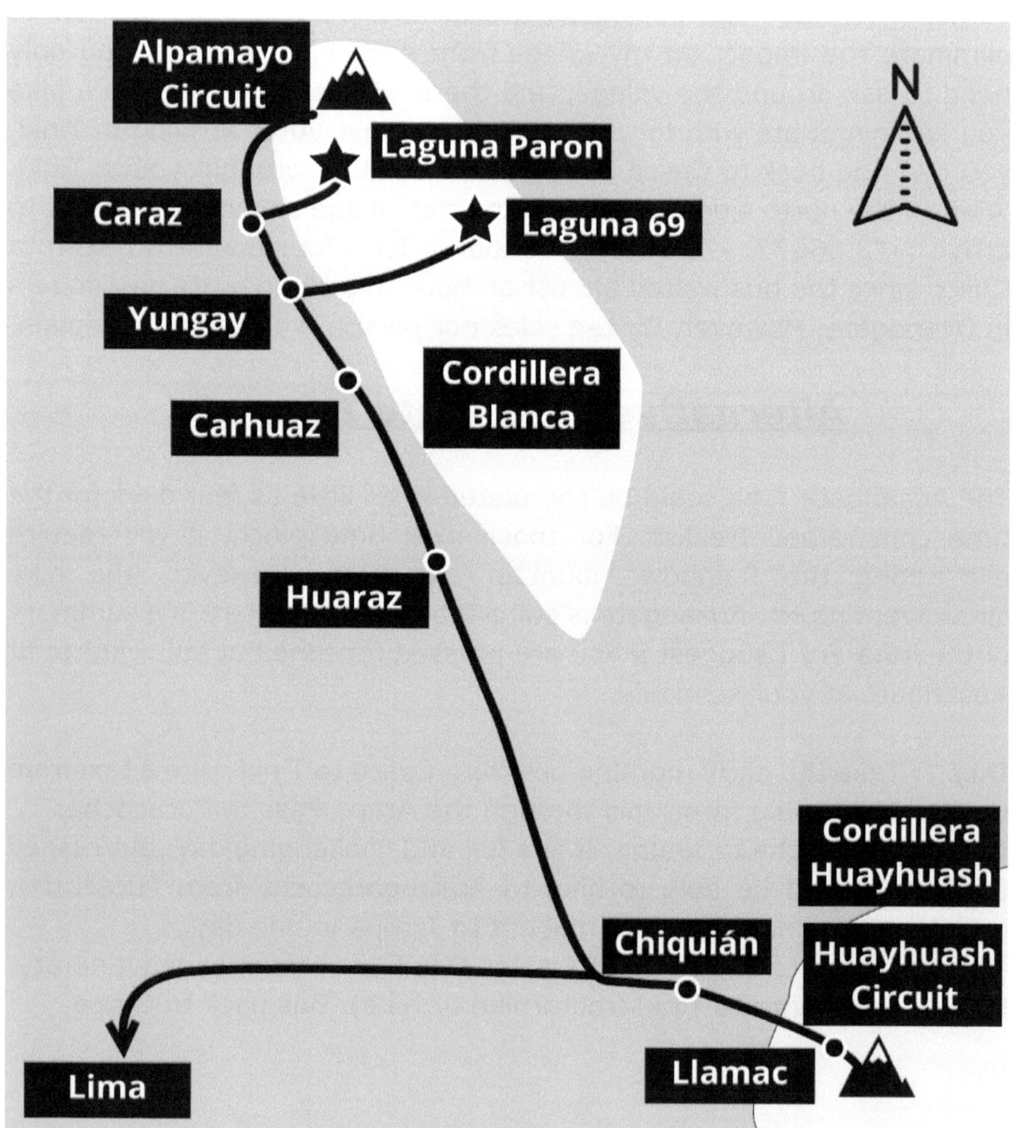

Huayhuash Circuit

The best treks on Planet Earth force every trekker to pay the price for its gifts. Every view, every moment of wonder, is earned. Nothing on the Huayhuash Circuit comes for free. The Huayhuash (pronounced "why-wash") is a physically demanding adventure that will test your ferocity, dedication, and command of the trail. But those that can earn a taste of this wonder will be privileged to witness the most spectacular scenery and what for me is the overall best trek I have ever completed. The Huayhuash Circuit will allow you to set your eyes upon some of the best mountain scenery South America has to offer.

The Huayhuash Circuit is home to some of Peru's tallest mountains, including Yerupajá, towering to 21,768 feet, and the Siula Grande at 20,814 feet made famous by Joe Simpson's thrilling climbing survival tale *Touching the Void*. To be in the presence of these monsters is mesmerizing and inspiring. Every view on the Huayhuash is earned with thigh-burning ascents at altitudes as high as 16,818 feet. The extreme harshness of the towering peaks that scatter this range are sculptures of the gods. Every day of the Huayhuash will blow you away with its pristine scenery. You will hike alongside the most beautiful turquoise lagunas, walk amongst giants that tower this range, and soak in nature that cannot be imagined.

It won't surprise me if you have never heard of the Huayhuash Circuit. I had never heard of this incredible paradise until digging deep into different online resources. The Huayhuash Circuit was initially not on my itinerary because it appeared too tremendous of a beast for me to tackle by myself. Blog after blog warned how trekking the Huayhuash is too hard to be completed independently. The logistics of getting there, the duration of the trek, and the incessant grind seemed like too big an apple for me to bite off. If I had listened to these warnings, I would have missed out on what was, without a doubt, the pinnacle trek of my Peruvian adventure.

The truth is that this trek, especially the route I completed, was tough to do independently. I would only recommend completing this trek completely independent of a guide service for highly experienced and well acclimated hikers. My first adventure on the Huayhuash was subsequent to completing two other high altitude Peruvian hikes so my body was well adjusted. However, any trekker with multi-day backpacking experience can complete it. The pros and cons of hiking alone versus a guided tour are exacerbated on the Huayhuash because there is such a rich variety of itineraries and severe topography. The longevity of the trek adds the extra burden on independent hikers who will be responsible for hauling all the food and gear they need for the entire seven to ten days.

Two of my three companions elected to join a tour company for the Huayhuash Circuit, and both had a fantastic time. They loved having the luxury of only having to carry a day pack throughout, not being responsible for navigation or logistics, and the social camaraderie of hiking alongside a group. It was reasonably priced, about $350 for a nine-day guided trek. For many hikers, a guided tour will be the way to go. *The only way to get a price this reasonable on a Huayhuash tour is not to seek a reservation until you arrive in Huaraz.* Otherwise, you will pay upwards to $3,000 for the same thing when booked abroad. My recommendation remains that hiking independently is optimal for increased flexibility. We completely changed our itinerary halfway through the hike after engaging with a local guide. This would not have been possible if we were another ant along for the ride.

When you study the Huayhuash Trail Map, it is evident that there are a ton of variations possible. Every alteration to the itinerary will pose its pros and cons. The standard Huayhuash Circuit makes a full loop around the entire circuit, skipping the spine of trails that run down its center. Our adventure to the Huayhuash Circuit took us off the beaten path from the conventional route and up through the center of the trek providing some breathtaking scenery. The way that we followed is known as the Alpine Trail within the Huayhuash range. This path covers territory that guided tours will not. The Alpine Trail posed dangers to us that would not be appropriate for unprepared and inexperienced hikers. Glacier crossings, loose rocks, and tricky descents might make my itinerary not fit for you, and depending on the current conditions, it might not be possible. However, I would not share the details of my recommended course if I were not confident that it could safely be done by those with proper experience. I seek to provide complete transparency about the risks associated with the path and give you an understanding of modifications you can make. This guide will outline the itinerary we chose to complete, and thoroughly explain alternatives you may wish to consider.

Logistics

The Huayhuash Circuit is a loop that starts at the Quartelhuain trailhead up at 13,652 feet and ends in the village of Llamac down at 10,712 feet. The trek can be completed in as few as seven days but could be

extended for the great explorers to two weeks. Technically, you could complete the trek in either direction, but I recommend starting in Quartelhuain so that you don't initiate the trek with a brutal uphill climb from Llamac.
Huaraz is the gateway to the Huayhuash Circuit. From Huaraz, it is a four to seven-hour ride to get to the circuit depending on how you get there. You have two options to consider for transportation to the circuit: public or private transport. The challenge with public transportation for the Huayhuash Circuit is that no bus will take you to the trailhead. The closest you can get to Quartelhuain via public transportation is the small village called Pocpa. Turismo Nazario operates a bus to Chiquián very early in the morning out of Huaraz, where you can connect to Llamac and Pocpa. Then you would have to walk along the dirt road that leads up to Quartelhuain. Private transportation will be a bit more expensive, but it has the consequential advantage of taking you all the way to the trailhead and avoiding meaningless stress on your legs. On my return journey to the Huayhuash, we secured a 4-hour taxi ride for 500 soles one way from Huaraz to Quartelhuain. This was by far the fastest and most convenient way to get to the trail, but obviously with a big price tag. Be aware that the Huaraz taxis aren't technically supposed to travel outside the city limits. You should plan to arrive at Quartelhuain before sunset. We arrived at night and got lucky that a local in Pocpa was available to let us through the entrance gate that was closed.

My budget recommendation for getting to the Huayhuash Circuit is to solicit a ride from one of the many tour companies in Huaraz that may have an extra seat. We walked around to every tour agency in town the day before we left until we could find one that had empty seats in their van. There is a little bit of risk with this method because they won't commit the seat to you until they are sure they won't receive a full tour fare paying customer. For us, this meant we didn't know if we would have a seat until 20:00 the night before we left. We ended up getting lucky, but the worst case would have been not getting a ride with the company and instead going with the public transportation option. This ride cost 60 soles per person (~$19). The public bus option might save you $10, but the convenience of not having to deal with a transfer in Chiquián and getting a ride directly to the trailhead is worth it.

Taking public transportation back to Huaraz from Llamac at the end of the trek is much easier than getting to Llamac from Huaraz. As soon as we descended to the village, there was a local waiting to show us where we could buy our tickets for the bus that goes straight from Llamac back to Huaraz for 25 soles (-10.19788, -77.03258). This bus leaves Llamac at 10:00 and is the only one available per day. Check with a local tour company the current bus schedule in Huaraz before departing.

Purchase and pack everything that you need for the trek in Huaraz. Make sure to pack plenty of small bills to pay the periodic tolls throughout the trek because the local collectors seldom have change to provide. There aren't any resupply options throughout the Huayhuash Circuit. Huayllapa is the closest thing to a village that you may cross before reaching Llamac. But it only has extremely basic items and should not be relied upon. You most certainly won't find an ATM.

If you are trekking independently, the only locations with access to transportation to exit the trail are Huayllpa, Llamac, and Pocpa. All other sites along the trail are not road accessible. Our return journey unfortunately forced us to end our hike early and exit the trail at Huayallpa. Public transportation from Huayllpa to Huaraz requires three different bus transfers that, according to the locals, are very unreliable. We ended up hiring a local to drive us the whopping nine hours all the way from Huayallpa to Huaraz for 1000 soles. It was a grueling drive down and around the mountains. Unless you are very pressed for time, I would highly recommend planning on completing the hike and exiting at Llamac. But it's always good to know your options when embarking on a physically demanding trek.

Permits and Reservations

There are no advanced permits required for the Huayhuash Circuit. However, there are tickets that you will need to purchase along the way. Locals will stop you at particular spots near or at the campgrounds to collect a small fee ranging from five to thirty soles per person. It was not clear if these fees were only due to us being independent trekkers, or if the guides of groups pay the fees for their clients. The fees increased significantly from my original journey in 2019 to my return two years later, so make sure to bring a lot of cash in small bills because you most certainly will not find an ATM anywhere outside of Huaraz. Depending on which route you choose, you will encounter anywhere from six to nine fee collection spots. The money helps support local maintenance of the trail and encourages greater safety and accountability of the area. Each ticket you pay for should come with a carbon copy. Make sure to keep it for proof of payment. You may be required to present this to authorities or pay a fine.

Costs

Item	Cost (Soles)
High-Quality Topographic Map	80 (2019)
Tolls 2022: Pocpa - 40pp, Janca - 40pp, Carhuacocha - 30pp, Huayhuash - 30pp, Huallypa- 50pp (even if you are not staying overnight), Cutatambo - 30pp	Bring at least 300 soles per person!
Private Bus from Huaraz to Quartelhuain	60 pp (2019)
Private Taxi from Huaraz to Quartelhuain	500 total (2022)
Public Bus from Llamac to Huaraz	25 pp (2019)
Private Taxi from Huayllpa to Huaraz	900 pp total (2022)
Lima to Huaraz Bus	75 pp

Huayhuash Overview Trail Map

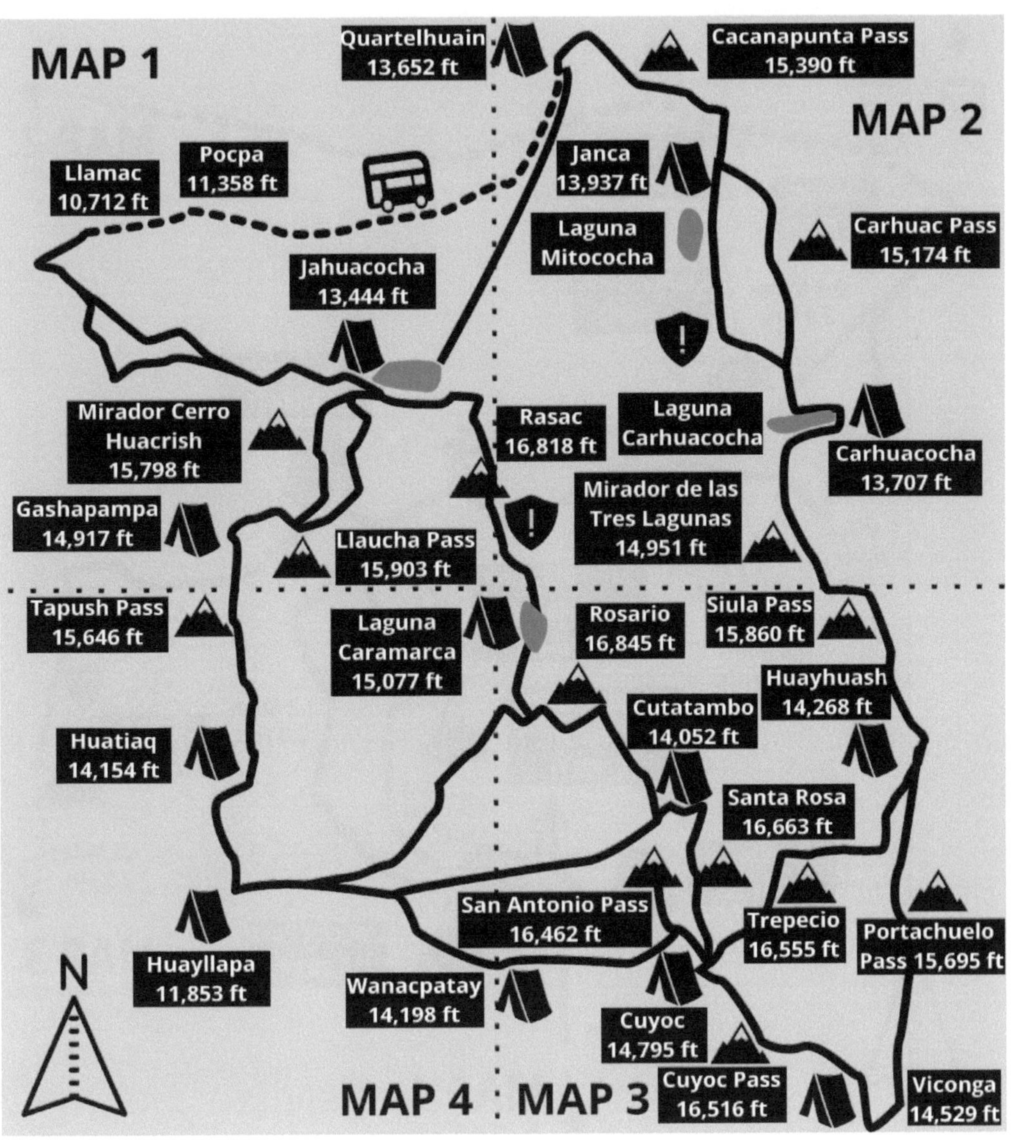

Huayhuash Trail Map 1

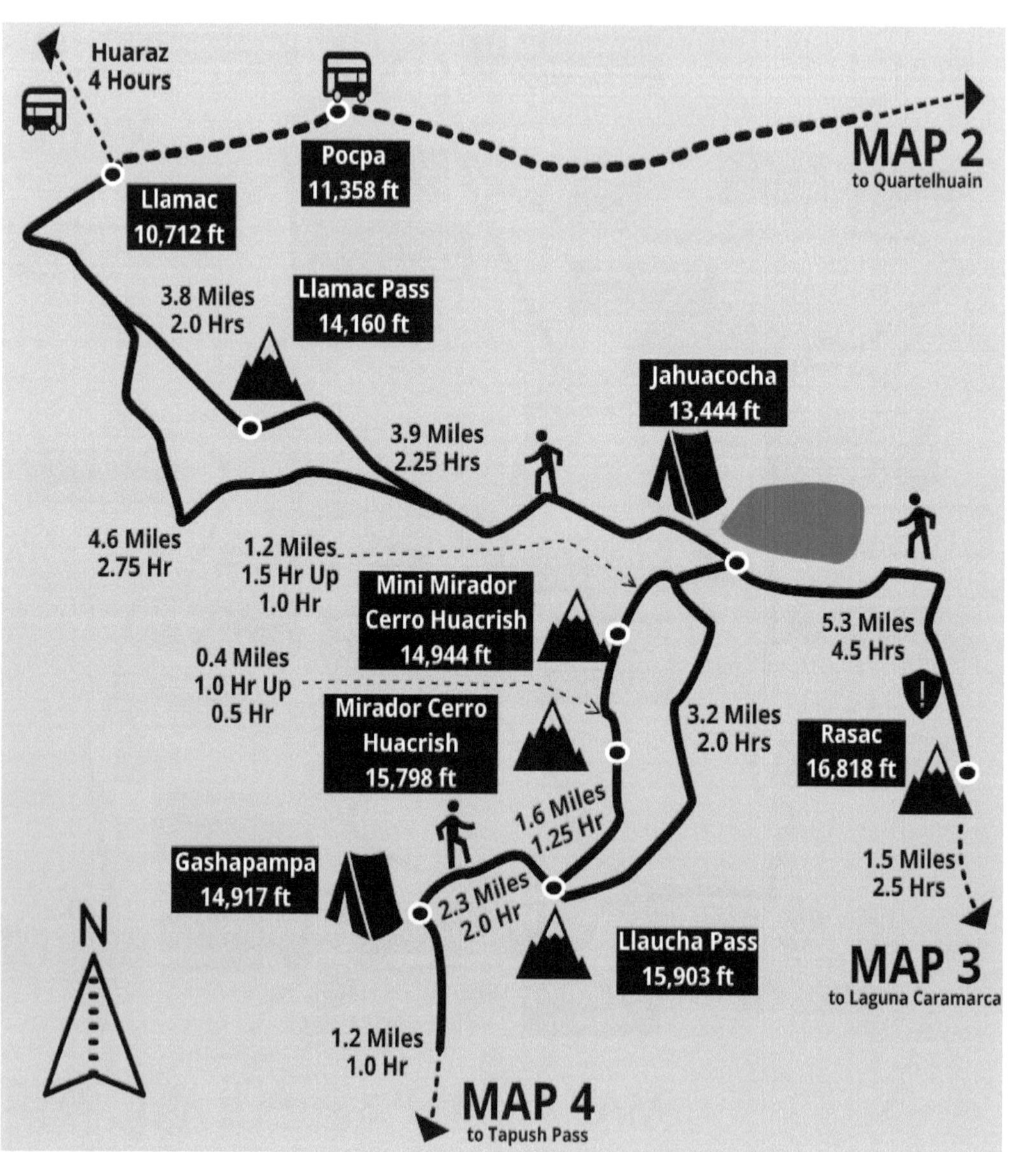

Huayhuash Trail Map 2

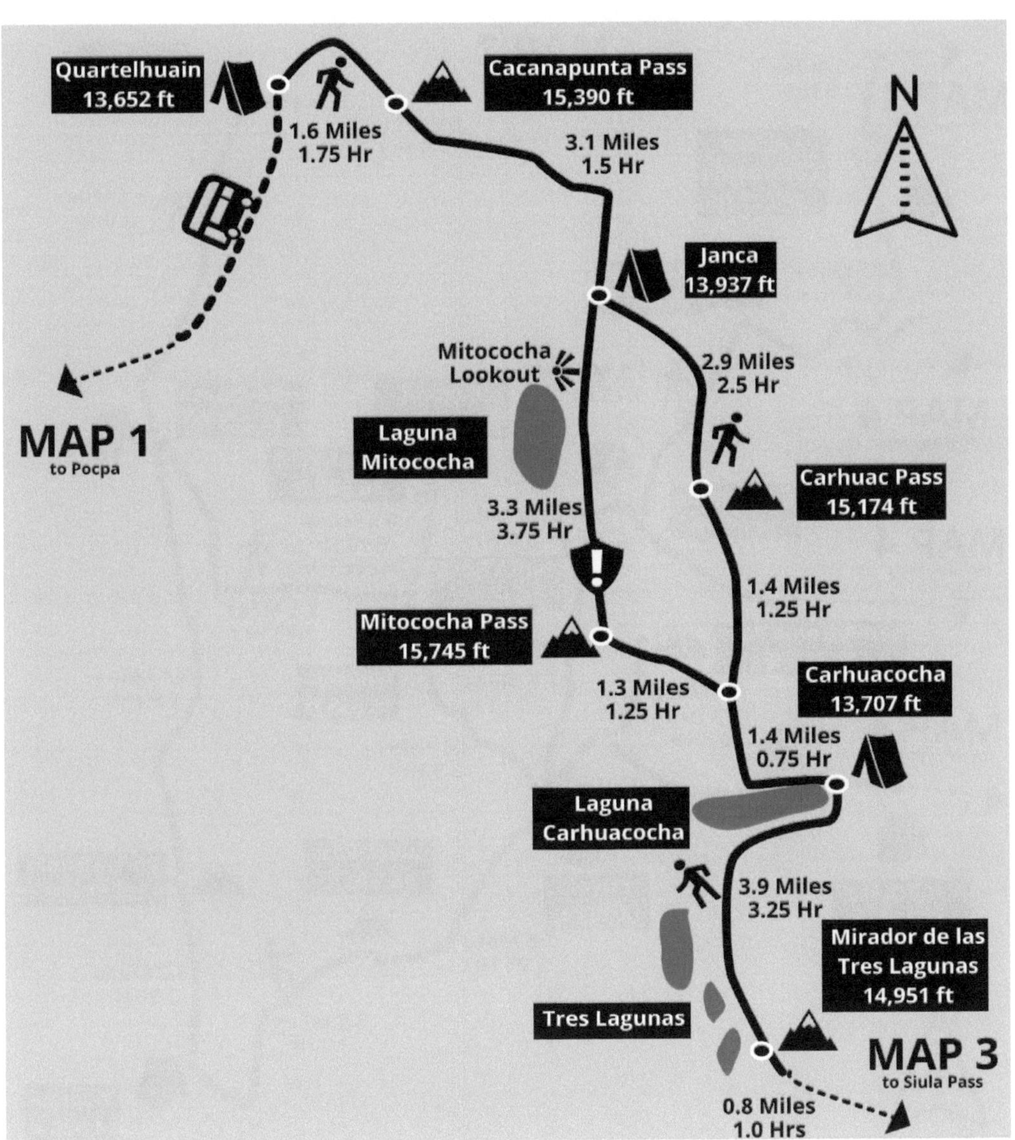

Huayhuash Trail Map 3

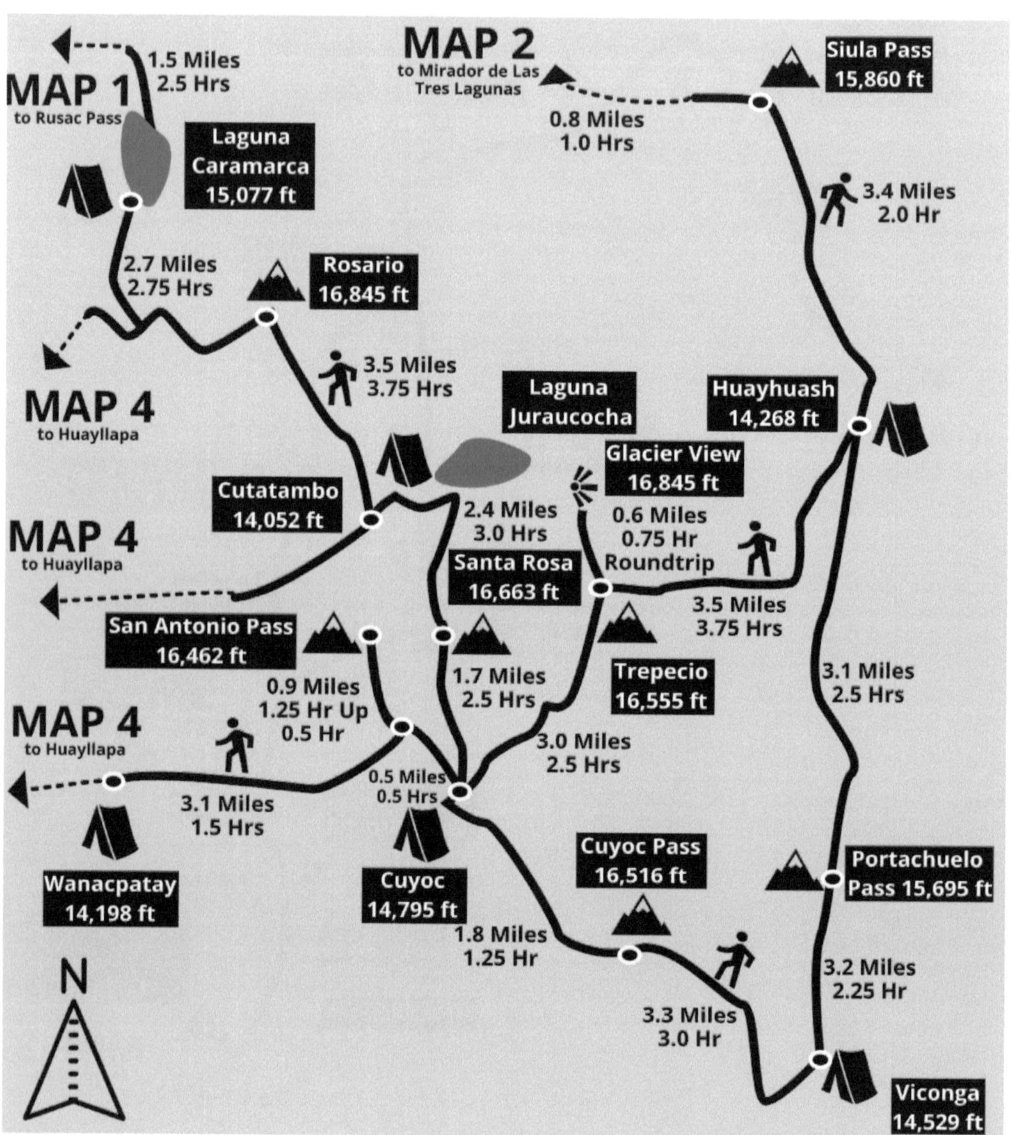

Huayhuash Trail Map 4

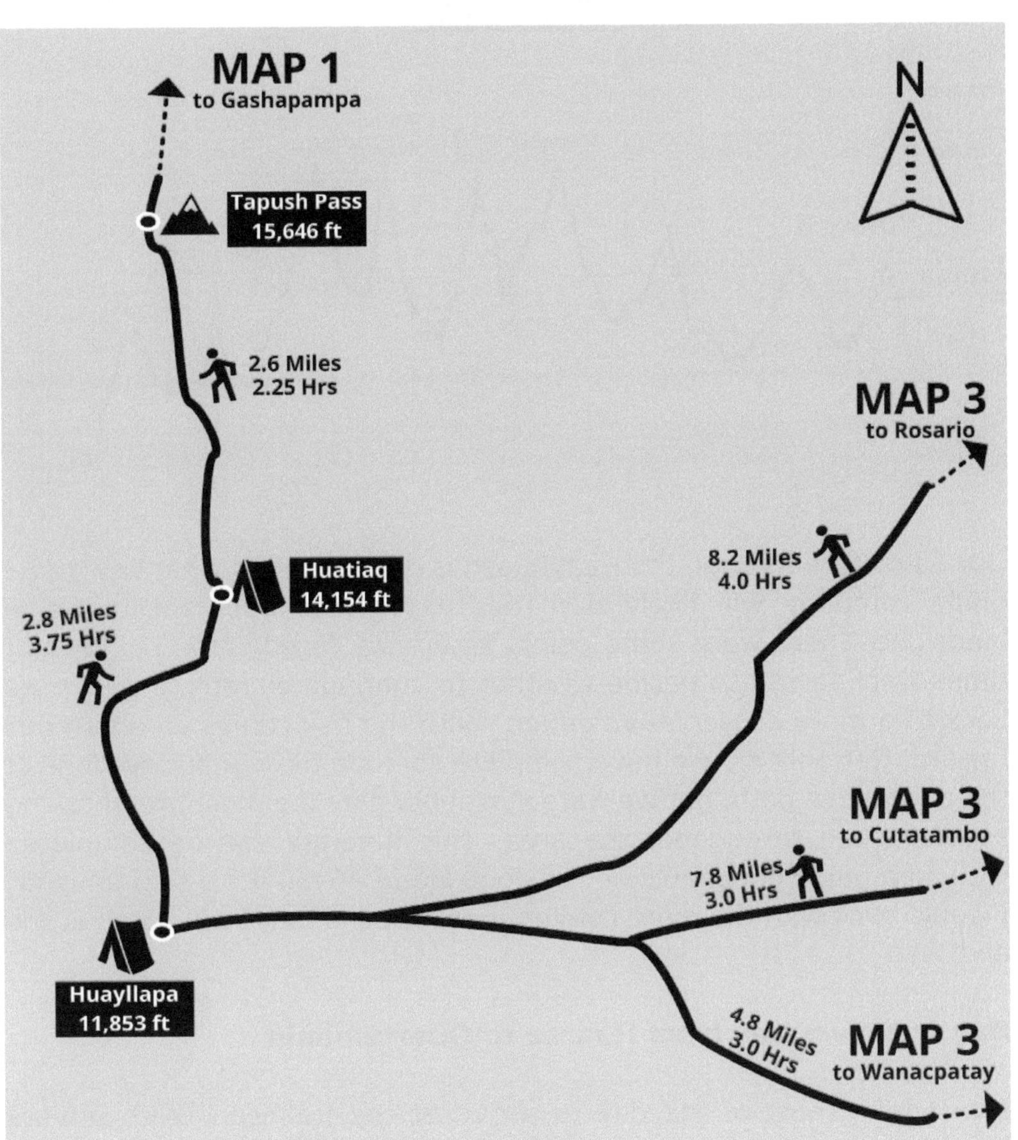

9 Day Alpine Trail Itinerary – The Road Less Traveled

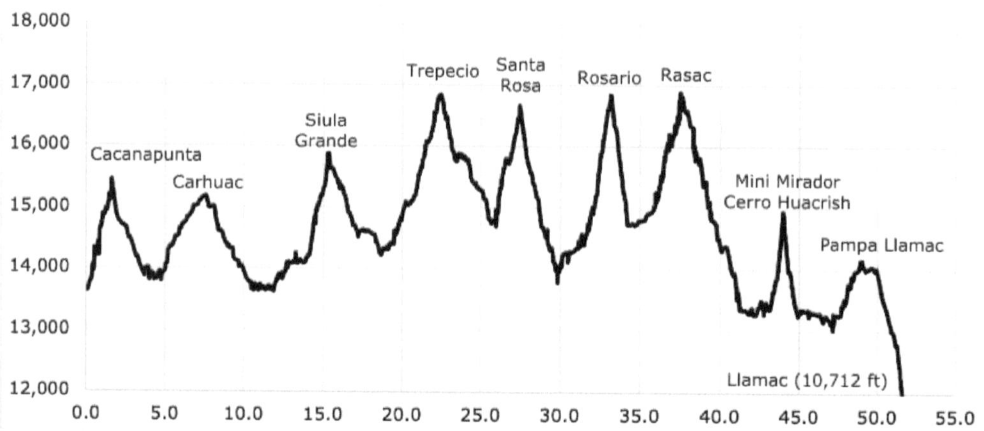

Our adventure through the Huayhuash is different than what any travel guide company will likely do. The reason was apparent to us in hindsight. There were some points where we faced some risk and at times were forced to decide whether to continue or retrace our route back to a more conservative option. With the risk comes an enormous reward. Not only did we have complete solitude throughout sections of the alternative path, but we were surrounded by the most breathtaking scenery seen throughout the area. This itinerary can be completed without a guide but should not be done alone. If you are a solo traveler, I would stick with the more conventional options that I will detail at the end.

Day 0: Travel Day from Huaraz to Quartelhuain

It will take most of the day to arrive at the trailhead. With private transportation, we did not arrive at the trailhead until 14:30. If you are taking public transit, your arrival at the trailhead will likely be even later. On our trek, we started the hike towards Janca on the first day.

I don't recommend this because we couldn't make it there before sunset and had to set up camp in a rogue spot on the side of the trail. Stay and camp at Quartelhuain to prepare for the epic journey ahead. Quartelhuain does not provide any amenities but there is an accessible river.

Quartelhuain Trailhead: 13,652 feet

Day 1: Quartelhuain to Janca via Cacanapunta Pass

***Elevation profile is for combining Day 1 and 2...I recommend splitting this into two days.**

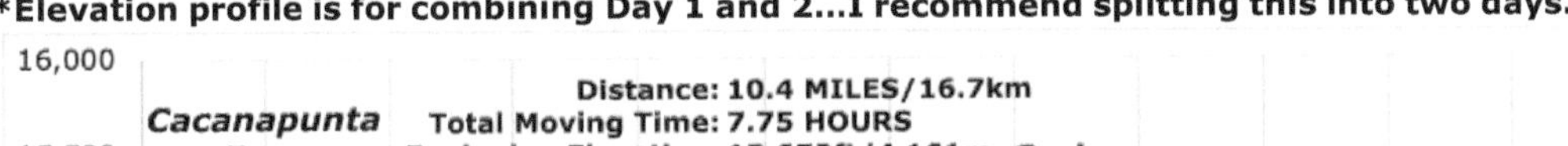

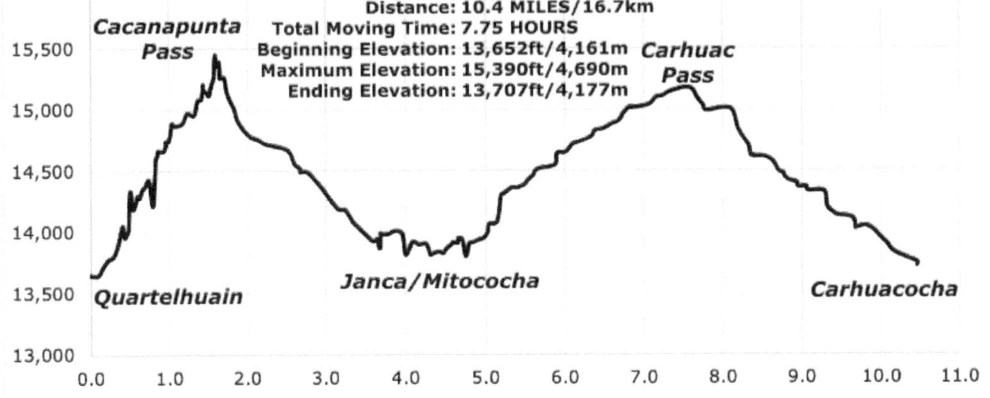

Day one is the first of many choices you'll have to make regarding your Huayhuash itinerary. Two passes separate Quartelhuain from one of the prettiest campsites you will ever set you tent upon, Carhuacocha. If the Huayhuash Circuit is your first major trek in Peru at high altitude, or you wouldn't consider being at peak hiking shape, you should consider splitting this day into two smaller chunks to better acclimate to the higher altitude and the feeling of having a full pack on your back again. It is possible to get from Quartelhuain all the way to Carhuacocha in one day, but unless you are extremely fit and accustomed to this type of terrain, I'd recommend splitting it in two. On the return journey we did trek from Quartelhuain to Carhuacocha in one day. We were so exhausted we ended up having to take a rest day the following day to recover. Plan to stay in Janca on the first night on trail. If I'm wrong and you get there early and are still feeling fresh, you can always continue to Carhuacocha and gain a day.

From Quartelhuain Campground, Start heading northwest towards the steep ascent to the top of the Cacanapunta Pass. The steep incline and rate of ascent make this a challenging climb. Over just 1.6 miles you will gain over 1,700 feet. After you have gained all this elevation, it will all be lost on the way to Janca. The 3.1 miles down to the Janca Campground area is an easy to follow trail that descends southeast halfway up from the river and the top of the ridgeline to the south. Either choose to stop here for the rest of the day or continue another 4-5 hours to Carhuacocha.

Day 2: Janca via Carhuacocha vis Carhuac Pass

From the Janca Campground, there are at least two different paths to choose to get to Carhuacocha. *Heading straight south uphill leads to the Mitococha Pass, which was incredibly beautiful but led to an overly risky scramble that I do not recommend to anybody*. I recommend staying on the eastern pass, which is the more popular route. This will lead to the more gradual but still challenging ascent to the top of the

Carhuac Pass at 15,174 feet. The trail continues to be straightforward navigationally to the Carhuacocha Campground. Carhuacocha is a mesmerizing lake with incredible mountains in the background. A fresh dip in its glacial waters was precisely the refreshing wakeup that my body needed after a full day on the trail. The northeast and southeast corners of the lake provide areas where you can set up a tent. The first area you will reach is the northeast corner of the lake. The ten area is elevated high above the water on the northeast side, and there is a convenient water pump that can supply you with untreated water. If you arrive earlier in the day and have energy to push an extra 15 minutes, I'd recommend staying at the campground on the southeastern corner of the lake on the water's edge, which would save you time on Day 3 and offers a better view in my opinion. But if you arrive at the northeastern camp and need to quickly set up camp that spot offers great views as well.

Carhuacocha Campground: 13,707 feet

Day 3: Carhuacocha to Huayhuash Campground via Siula Pass

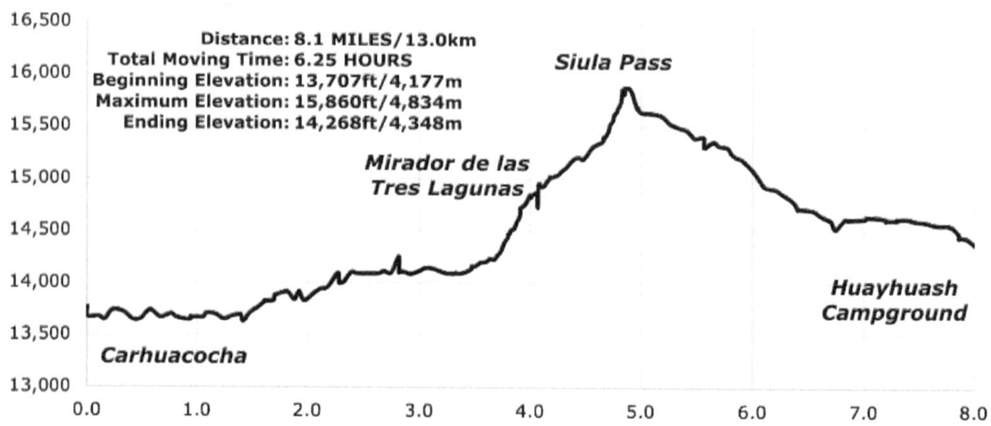

Few places earn the right to make the cover of a trekking guide. Day 3 is home to what remains to be the most beautiful sight that I have ever seen. The Mirador de las Tres Lagunas is the most wonderful vista with jagged peaks, massive glaciers, and the deepest blue lakes coming together like a dream. Part of the joy from Day 3 is derived from the challenge of reaching this natural wonder. Mileage is an inappropriate metric to describe Day 3. With over 2,100 feet of elevation gain, only trekkers with real grit deserve to bathe in this incomparable scenery.

The day's trek begins by hiking clockwise around the southern shore of Laguna Carhuacocha until reaching the southwest corner. If you camped on the closer, northern shore, stay hiking high and towards the water from the outhouse to navigate to the other side of the lake. From the southwestern corner of the lake, the trail heads south, and the gradient starts to increase. The trail is obvious all the way to the first lookout along Laguna Gangrajanca, which is the largest of the three Lagunas that make up the Tres Lagunas. It took us 1 hour and 45 minutes to hike from the campground to the first mirador. This spot is great for a mild snack break but save your major break for the real Mirador de las Tres Lagunas further ahead. After you hike south past the second lake, the trail starts to get quite steep and through some more dense flora than characteristic of the previous trail. Even when your legs are burning from the mighty uphill you face on this segment, keep pushing on until you have reached the coveted Mirador de las Tres Lagunas (-10.28489, -76.86452). Plan on spending a full break at this stop to completely absorb the majestic beauty of the Siula Grande and Yurpajá giants towering over the three beautiful turquoise lakes.

Mirador de las Tres Lagunas: 14,951 feet

The uphill trekking for the day doesn't end at the Mirador de las Tres Lagunas. Leave the mirador early enough to complete the three to four hours of hiking remaining on the day but not before taking a memory card full of pictures. I underestimated the extent of hiking left to do after the mirador. From the mirador, the trail goes uphill towards the southeast direction. You will go uphill, cross over a short flat section, and meet a steep rock face staring you down as you try to ascend to 15,860 feet reaching the Siula Pass. It will take about an hour to reach the Siula Pass from the Mirador de las Tres Lagunas depending on your pace. Do not underestimate this ascent. It is an extremely steep push to earn almost equitable views as the previous mirador.

Siula Pass: 15,860 feet

The section after the Siula Pass is the only navigationally difficult part of the day. The trail turns south and keeps you guessing regarding which ridge you should be hiking on. We had to do a bit of backtracking and meandering to eventually find the sure trail to camp. Keep your aim towards the western side of Laguna Carnicero. Once you get to the lake, the path becomes clear to the Huayhuash Campground. After two hours of hiking from the Siula Pass, you will reach the end of the day at Huayhuash Campground. There isn't a step along this day's hike that isn't spectacular. Cherish this day and get ready for the next step in the adventure. The Huayhuash campground provides running non potable water and an outhouse.

Day 4: Huayhuash to Cuyoc Campground via Trepecio Pass

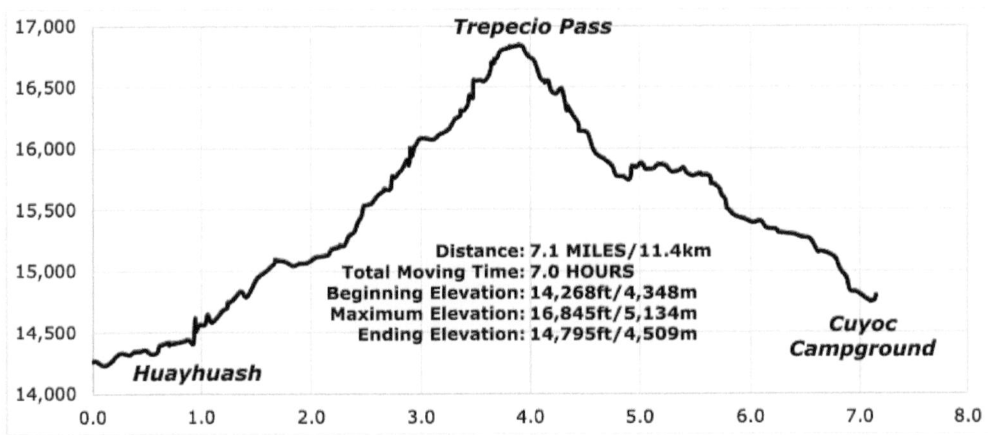

Day 4 is the first opportunity for you to deviate from the crowd and choose the road less traveled. Our original plan was to go the conventional route over the Portachuelo Pass, ending at the Viconga Campground where hot springs await. But as we discussed our strategy with a local guide, he convinced us to follow him and his group over the Trepecio Pass instead. He asserted that the views going through this pass were far superior to going the route through Viconga. If you go through the Trepecio Pass, you will miss out on the hot springs at Viconga, but the superior scenery is worth it. Plus, you save an entire day with this shortcut. Most of the tour groups hike the Viconga route, so if you want to escape the crowds, this alternative is the way to go. During my research for the trip, I had read about the Trepecio Pass option, but all accounts sounded as if the route was extremely complicated to navigate. This ended up being far from the truth. The Trepecio Pass is physically demanding, but we found no significant navigational challenges.

From the Huayhuash Campground, hike high on the right (western) side of the ridge. The trail is hard to find immediately but will become clear as you continue south towards Laguna Barrosacocha. You should be heading for the western side of the laguna (-10.3484, -76.85081). Take a rest at this point, then head almost directly west across the flat fields. Study the picture below and see where the trail up to the pass is. As you get closer to the uphill section, this trail that scars the face becomes obvious. Once you find the start of the trail, it is easy navigation to the summit of the pass.

View of the Trepecio Pass Trail from Rest Point (-10.3484, -76.85081)

Without speaking with the local guide, we certainly would have missed out on the highlight of the day. Finishing the almost 2,300 feet of elevation gain up to the Trepecio Pass will make you feel like you've reached the ultimate summit of the day. But the real summit is a scramble from the pass up to the Trepecio Glacier. When you get to the peak of the Trepecio Pass, scramble up the rocks heading north for about twenty minutes until you reach the Trepecio Glacier. Some groups walked onto the glacier. We settled for the incredible viewpoint overlooking the Trepecio Mountain and its massive glacier. Even though this side trip adds an additional 45 minutes of hiking and 300 feet of elevation gain, it is worth it.

Views of the Trepecio Glacier: 16,845 feet

From the Trepecio Pass, the trail descends towards a gorgeous set of lakes with Mt. Puscantrurpa in the background. It is a bit of a rollercoaster hike going up and down until it finally makes a big descent to the Cuyoc Campground. This section of the hike was challenging after a long morning ascent to the pass.

Path Connecting Trepecio Pass and Cuyoc Campground

I highly recommend completing the Trepecio Pass over going to Viconga and making sure you allow time to visit the glacier. Our experience completing this segment was fantastic, but not without a significant physical challenge. It took almost four hours for us to get to the top of the Trepecio Pass from Huayhuash Campground. The Cuyoc Campground is one of the most massive camping spots where you certainly will be sharing space with other tour groups. You will have great water access and even a flushing toilet.

Day 5: Cuyoc to Cutatambo via Santa Rosa Pass

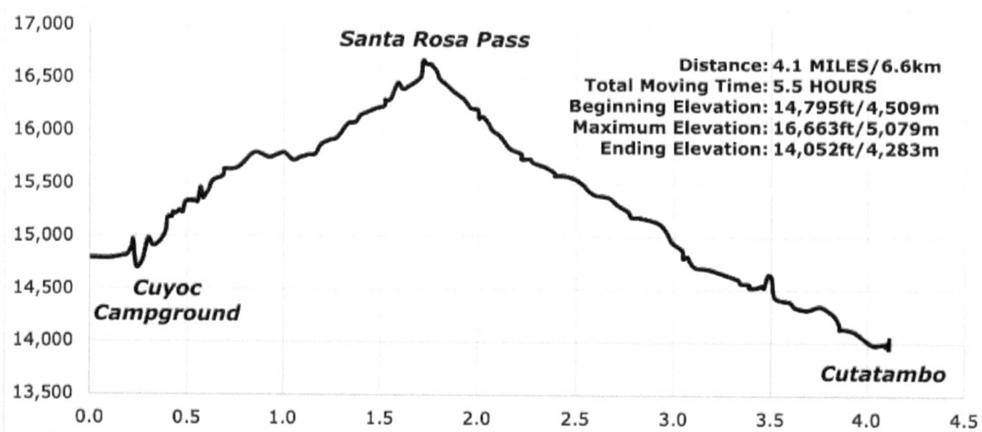

Even though this is the shortest day of the Huayhuash Circuit, it doesn't make it the easy or lackluster. The fact that many trekkers skip the Santa Rosa Pass entirely and continue west along the valley towards Huayllapa baffles me. They are missing out on one of the great highlights of the Huayhuash Circuit. From the Cuyoc Campground, there are two parallel uphill paths to similar passes. On the western side is the San Antonio Pass hovering to 16,462 feet. This is an option if you would like to hike up and then back down and onto Huayllapa. It might be possible to hike from the San Antonio Pass to Cutatambo, but every guide I spoke to shut down that idea because of how dangerous the northern side of the pass is. Each guide that I interviewed recommended the equally beautiful and much safer Santa Rosa Pass.

From the Cuyoc Campground, the ascent up to the Santa Rosa Pass is a two-hour grind testing your physical and mental toughness. The only challenge navigationally is finding where it starts. I'd recommend following a tour group at least until you get on the trail. You will start heading back towards the Trepecio Pass but then curve uphill and north towards the Santa Rosa Pass. There is a serious false summit after an hour of hiking that will tempt you to believe that the hardest part of the day is over. Continue past this flat terrain and towards the next steep uphill face that is scarred by the trail leading up to the summit. After countless switchbacks, the Santa Rosa Pass sneaks up on you and reveals a breathtaking view of Laguna Juraucocha and the Sarapo, Carnicero, and Siula Grande mountains.

Santa Rosa Pass: 16,663 feet

Take your time at this summit and enjoy the descent towards Juraucocha. We spent a couple of hours at an incredible spot above the lake that offered amazing views of the enormous lake up close before finally heading to Cutatambo (-10.33732, -76.89283). To get down to Cutatambo, follow the ridgeline west overlooking the lake and then take

any cut in the path down the southern face away from the lake. We mistakenly followed a path north descending to the water's edge. This path ended up being a much more robust way to go.
There is also the option of planning to make it to Huayllapa after Cutatambo. The problem with this idea is that you will be skipping the hike up to the Rosario Pass, which I think is a must-see and it rushes the day. My companions traveling with the tour company completed this full day to Huayllapa but couldn't spend adequate time enjoying the views of Juraucocha like we did.

As mentioned in the introduction, injuries on my return journey forced us to exit the trail early at Huayllapa. We hiked through smoggy saturated trail along the valley from Cuyoc passed the Huanacpatay campground down to Huayllapa. This took us about five hours total walking before we took our private transportation to Huaraz. I would only recommend going this route if conditions or extenuating circumstances force you to exit the Huayhuash at Huayllapa.

Day 6: Cutatambo to Laguna Caramarca via Rosario Pass

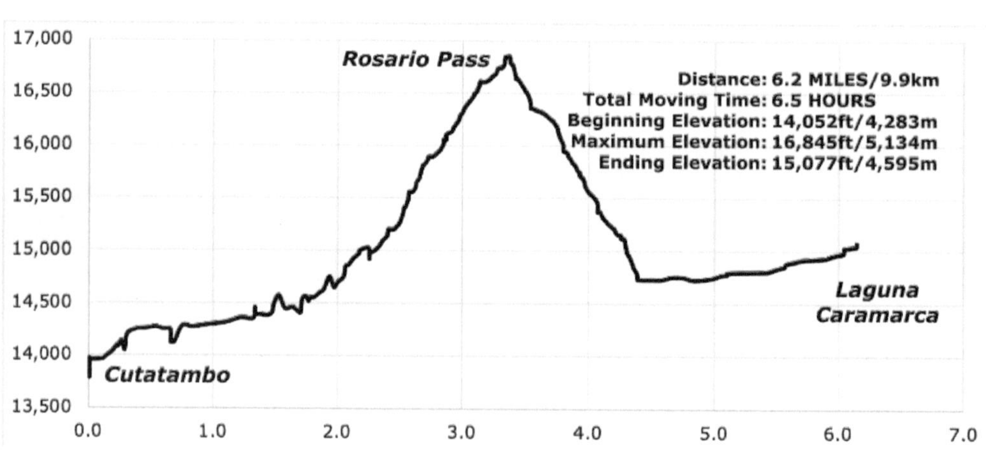

The Cutatambo Campground is the start of what I would call the actual Alpine Trail within the Huayhuash Circuit. We found absolute solitude from Cutatambo all the way until the end of the next day when we arrived at Jahuacocha. This day includes a lot of challenging navigation where trails disappear, and you must completely forge your own path to the top. From Cutatambo, find the trail uphill almost due north, staying west of Juraucocha. The trail meanders gradually uphill in the trough of the valley and eventually pushes you higher up on the western face of the valley. Take your first break at the fantastic Siula Grande Viewpoint (-10.31431, -76.91507). You have unbelievable views of the Siula Grande mountain and Sarapococha.

Sarapococha Mirador with Siula Grande

After this viewpoint, the trail disappears. The path used to continue further north along the same gradient but is no longer passable due to a mudslide. From the viewpoint, start hiking steeply uphill southwest until you reach the top of the ridge. This is an exercise of choosing your own path because there isn't any defined trail. Keep your aim on the top ridgeline without drifting too far south. Look for the stacked boulders marking the top of the ridgeline and then follow it northwest until you reach the pass.

View of Ascent Leading to the Rosario Pass. Look for the Stacked Boulder. (-10.3181, -76.92282)

From this viewpoint with the stacked boulders, it is relatively easy to find the Rosario Pass by continuing northwest along the ridgeline and ascending another 300 feet. Take a well-deserved lunch break at the summit and enjoy the incredible 360-degree views filled with stunning mountain ranges. The best part for us was that we had the entire area all to ourselves.

Rosario Pass: 16,845 feet

After the Rosario Pass, it was a bit of a challenge reaching the valley that leads to Laguna Caramarca. First, you will have to descend an enormous boulder field with rocks small enough that you can run down if you have durable footwear. As you continue to lose more elevation, there is no definitive trail indicating if you should stay high on the eastern face of the valley or if you should fully descend to the base. We traversed high, heading north as long as we could but then went down another loose rock face to get to the valley floor. I recommend following whatever path you find that leads to the valley floor as directly as possible. We found herds of wild cows patrolling this valley leading up to the Laguna Caramarca. At this point, the lack of trail became pretty frustrating. You must persevere through the uncertainty and lack of guidance until you find the lake. In that mile leading up to the lake, stay on the east side of the valley and keep following different trails until you reach the finish line for the day. Laguna Caramarca is worth every ounce of grit and frustration it took to find over the course of a full day. The great Yerupajá and Rasac mountains surround this stunning lake and was all ours for the night.

Laguna Caramarca: 15,077 feet

Day 7: Laguna Caramarca to Jahuacocha via Rasac Pass

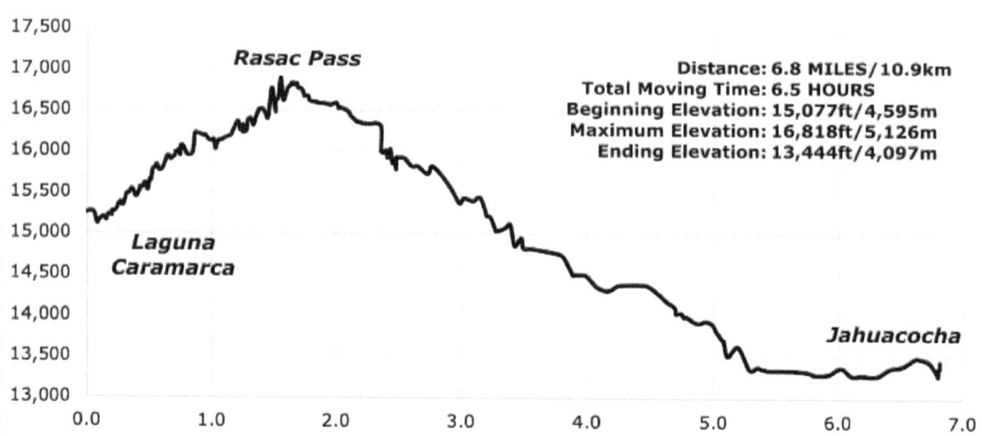

As explained in the introduction to the Huayhuash Circuit, the Alpine Trail has its risks that you need to be aware of. So far, everything described has been a safe pathway to get to the Laguna Caramarca. Regardless of whether you choose to follow the rest of the Alpine Trail after Laguna Caramarca, I wouldn't change my recommendation up until this point. The hike up to Rosario Pass and camping at Laguna Caramarca were extraordinary experiences I hope you can enjoy as well. There are two options available to you from Laguna Caramarca. First is the more conservative option of spending the day hiking back south down the valley until you reach Huayllapa and then hiking up to Huatiaq. The downside is losing a tremendous amount of elevation and adding an extra day.

The second option, which my group successfully completed, is to continue on the Alpine Trail north over a glacier, scramble up the Rasac Pass, and descend some precarious rocks to Jahuacocha. If you look at the Huayhuash Overview Trail Map, it is clear that this is a massive shortcut, and saves you from a tedious descent. The dangers associated with the segment first involve a traverse over a glacier to get to the Rasac Pass. Glaciers can be dangerous to cross because of their unknown structure. ***Hidden crevasses pose a great risk to anyone hiking without experience.*** The guide who recommended this route indicated we would only be on the glacier for ten minutes. We ended up walking up and across it for nearly two hours. Towards the top of the pass, we were faced with a problematic scramble that didn't require any climbing equipment but still was not a simple walk-up. There is always the option that you can hike north to the glacier and make the decision for yourself when you reach it. Overall, if you feel you have good hiking experience, proper safety judgment and are with a competent crew, you can complete this section. If you would rather avoid any unnecessary risk, are hiking alone, or experience poor weather conditions, take the valley route down to Huayllapa. The rest of this section will be dedicated to those wishing to complete the Alpine Trail.

From Laguna Caramarca, the trail follows the ridgeline on the west side of the lake for a solid hour until you reach the base of the glacier. Maps.me showed that the trail continued further up on the west side before actually crossing onto the glacier. We could not find any way up to the pass except for hiking straight up the expanse of the glacier. You don't need any crampons or ice axes, but trekking poles are a definite must for hiking this section. The glacier was soft enough that we could easily create our own switchback pattern and never feel slippery. You are aiming for the northwest corner of the glacier.

Ascent Towards the Rasac Pass

After reaching the summit of Rasac Pass, the descent is equally challenging with massive boulder fields, scarce trails and cairns to follow, and lots of grazing wildlife.

Viewpoint North of Rasac Pass (-10.2757, -76.93621)

From this viewpoint, the trail continues to the west before starting the descent to Barrosaccocha. The descent was tough but safe. There was only one spot before getting near Barrosaccocha where we had to take our packs off and backward climb down about ten feet of rock. Stay away from the upper ridge of Barrosaccocha even though some cairns indicate that it's the correct way (indicated by black x's in the picture above). Stay low on the west side instead. The trail up on the ridge is unstable and doesn't lead anywhere. There is a clear trail connecting Barrosaccocha to Rasaccocha, but then it once again it disappears. Once you get north of Rasaccocha, your goal is to hike to the west side of the next lake called Laguna Cochacotan. Herds of cattle use this land for grazing. Choose whatever path high or low that gets you to the western shore of Cochacotan.

After you pass Cochacotan, follow the river and valley down to the north. You need to find a place high on the river to cross to the east side. There was a good path on the western side but did not lead to a great place to cross the river. I recommend finding a place to cross this river to the east side as soon as possible. From the east side of the river, follow the cattle trail to the valley floor where you will see the giant Jahuacocha lake. The campground is located on the far west side of the lake. To get to the campground from the valley floor, find the trail by crossing over the network of rivers that flow to the lake near the southern shore and hike west until you find the wide-open stretch likely occupied by other tour groups.

This is an especially challenging day. Luckily, you can reward yourself with a bottle of coke or beer for sale at the Jahuacocha Campground. You will enjoy getting to tell the story of the thrilling adventure to everyone else who took the conventional route.

Day 8: Optional Day Hike to the Mini Mirador Cerro Huacrish

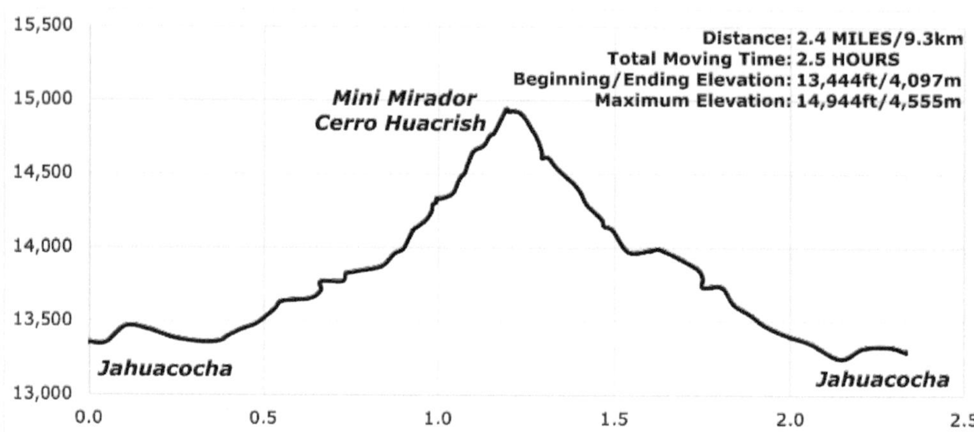

After seven intense days of hiking, enjoy a late morning wakeup at Jahuacocha, where you don't have to break down camp and go on a fantastic day hike to the Mini Mirador Cerro Huacrish. Follow the main dirt trail heading southwest and uphill from the campground. It is a well-defined trail that has been etched into the ground by line after line of donkeys. There is no marker indicating where you need to abandon the trodden path for an indistinct way up to the mirador. You should be able to see on up and to your right the rock formation shown below. The mirador is past this on the left-hand side. The trail becomes more pronounced the higher you ascend.

Ascent up to the Mini Mirador Cerro Huacrish

Once you reach the top of the viewpoint, you have the option to continue higher up towards the southwest another 900 feet of elevation to the true Mirador Cerro Huacrish (-10.24614, -76.97658). We were more than satisfied with the view we earned from this lower viewpoint and saw minimal marginal benefit of continuing further uphill (-10.24214, -76.97381). The lookout provided unbelievable views of Jahuacocha, and the fantastic Jirishanca mountain. The entire day trip takes about four hours round trip, giving you plenty of time to recover and prepare for the final leg. It would be a good idea to scout out the trail that heads to Llamac so that when you start before sunrise the next day, you have an enhanced sense of navigation. Get to sleep early, so you are prepared for an early wake up to complete the circuit.

Mini Mirador Huacrish: 14,944 feet

Day 9: Jahuacocha to Llamac. Bus back to Huaraz.

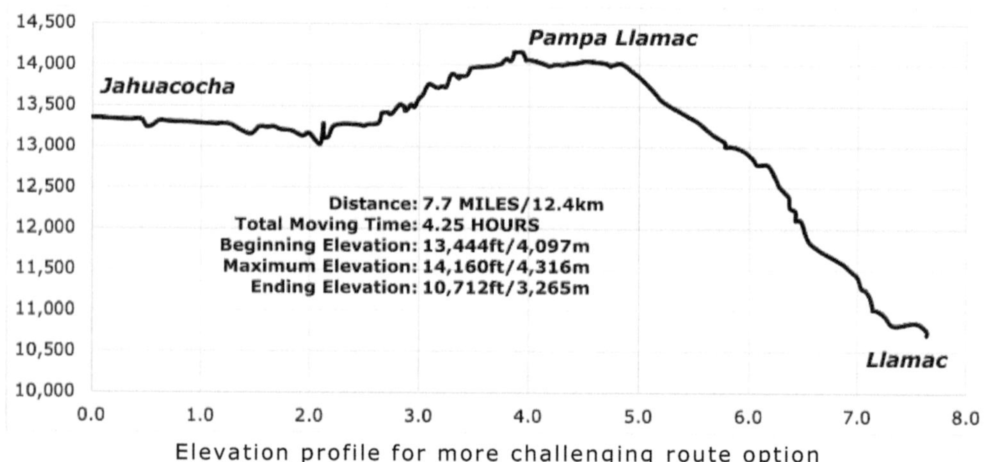

Elevation profile for more challenging route option

Your goal should be to arrive in Llamac by 09:30 so you comfortably make the bus that returns to Huaraz, which leaves between 10:00 and 10:30. For us, this required a 04:20 wakeup in the dark and starting to hike by 04:50. There are two options for completing the hike. The main trail takes you up to Pampa Llamac and ending with a knee killing descent to the village of Llamac. Alternatively, there is a much easier route that circumnavigates much of the uphill and downhill climbing. This fork is marked by a sign showing the path to the right to be towards

Llamac. That path leads to the more physically challenging route. If you stay left and ignore this sign, you can get to Llamac more easily. The hard trail did not offer any views that come close to what you've been spoiled by the last eight days, so I would probably recommend taking the easy way out to Llamac.

As you reach Llamac, head east towards the city center, and there will likely be a local offering to take you to the bus station to get your ticket (-10.19788, -77.03258). See the Logistics section for more details.

Summary of Alternate Conservative Itinerary

Days 1-6: Same as Alpine Trail, up until Laguna Caramarca
Day 7: Laguna Caramarca -> Huayllapa -> Huatiaq
Day 8: Huatiaq to Jahuacocha via Mirador Cerro Huacrish
Day 9: Same as Alpine Trail

Alpamayo Circuit

The Cordillera Blanca in Peru's northern Andes is an expansive playground with enough world-class hiking to last for decades. This mountain range is highlighted by Peru's tallest mountains, including the supreme Mt. Huascarán at 22,204 feet and Huandoy at 20,980 feet. Much of the area within the Cordillera Blanca is part of the Huascarán National Park. Nestled inside this mountain range live a network of extraordinary trails. Hikes of all durations and technical difficulty are available here. Of all the treks you can complete throughout the Cordillera Blanca, the Alpamayo Circuit will be the most mystical, challenging, and rewarding. This trek was my first completely solo multi-day backpacking experience. The mental and physical strain of hiking alone for eleven days straight was a humbling experience and taught me a lot about myself and my hiking style.

The most popular trek in this region is the four-day Santa Cruz Trek. Many hikers use the Santa Cruz Trek as a warmup for the Huayhuash Circuit. The Alpamayo Circuit is an extended version of the Santa Cruz trek, including all the same highlights as well as a tremendous amount of territory seldom experienced by visitors. Mt. Alpamayo may not be the tallest of the giants occupying this range, but at 19,551 feet, it stands out for its perfectly shaped pinnacle. Mountain climbers all over the world attempt to reach the summit of this mountain frequently named, "The Most Beautiful Mountain in the World."

The Alpamayo Circuit is a tale of two treks. The first section that overlaps with the Santa Cruz Trek is well trodden with numerous tour groups and donkeys carrying load upon load of gear. Here, you will have no issues whatsoever staying on the correct path and finding new friends to exchange adventure stories along the way. As soon as the path splits away from the "Santa Cruz Highway," it is an entirely different story. Many days will be characterized by complete solitude, nonexistent trails, and unmarked campgrounds. For some, this will be a welcome change from the typical buzz of people surrounding the world's greatest hikes. Still, others might struggle with the almost intoxicating intimacy with your conscience you achieve after so long by yourself. Navigation of the Alpamayo Circuit can be extremely frustrating for those without experience hiking in the wild. Certain sections of the circuit lack any trail, forcing you to use a mix of topographical maps, GPS, and instinct to find your way.

Hiking through the Alpamayo Circuit will expose you to some of the most beautiful scenery in the world. Challenging ascents up mountain passes are rewarded with breathtaking views reaching at most 16,500 feet in elevation. If you are forced to choose between the Huayhuash Circuit and the Alpamayo Circuit, choose the Huayhuash Circuit. The Alpamayo Circuit is a marathon of a hike that offers spectacular scenery but doesn't quite meet the beauty of the Huayhuash. Choose the Alpamayo Circuit if you seek greater solitude and wildness of the trail. Despite the navigational obscurity and intense longevity of the Alpamayo Circuit, it is a safe hike to complete without a whole lot of atypical risk.

Logistics

The Alpamayo Circuit is a giant horseshoe loop that will put over eighty miles under your feet. It takes eleven days to complete the full circuit but can be reduced to as little as nine days if you skip two of the optional day hikes. The two endpoints of the trek are the villages of Cashapampa and Hualcayán. Throughout the trek, there are two exit points in case you need to abort for any reason, including Pomabamba and Vaqueria. The Alpamayo Circuit can be hiked in either direction. My recommendation is to start the hike at Cashapampa and end at Hualcayán. The main problem with starting at Hualcayán is the ascent you will endure on the first day with a bursting-to-the-brim full pack. To get from Hualcayán to the first campsite will include almost 5,000 feet of elevation gain. My preference was to tackle this considerable elevation change as a descent at the end of the trip when my pack would be relatively lightweight. However, I can see two main advantages of starting in Hualcayán and ending at Cashapampa. First, getting transportation back to Caraz from Cashapampa is easier than from Hualcayán. More dependable public transportation arrives in Cashapampa than Hualcayán. It may be a better strategy to get private transportation from Caraz to take you to Hualcayán, and then when you end up at Cashapampa, there is a higher likelihood that you'll find a ride back to Caraz. The second advantage of starting in Hualcayán is that you will generally reach the passes earlier in the day, which might yield better conditions.

Another reason I recommend starting in Cashapampa is the fact that I prefer the opportunities to shorten the trek toward the end rather than at the beginning. The two different chances to reduce the total trek occur on the Hualcayán side. It is harder to evaluate if you should change the eleven-day hike to a nine-day hike on Day 2 rather than on Day 8 when you have had a lot of time to listen to your body and mind. The pacing of the hike and the increasing quality of views also makes me recommend the counter-clockwise direction. Both options are possible, and each has its pros and cons for you to consider.

Getting There

To get to Cashapampa, first you need to travel to Caraz. If you are cramming the days in, you can take the earliest collectivo from Huaraz to Caraz, and then transfer to another collectivo to take you to Cashapampa on the same day. I dislike stressful early mornings, so opted to travel to Caraz, stay overnight, and then the next day take the morning collectivo to Cashapampa. The collectivo station in Caraz is right next to the main produce market (-9.046265, -77.807173) and runs about every thirty minutes. It takes ninety minutes to travel from Caraz to Cashapampa via collectivo and costs 15 soles.

The best backpacking food, such as packaged meats, nuts, bars, and more, are found in the Huaraz supermarkets. Do not rely on finding anything besides produce in the markets of Caraz. You could reduce the amount of food you need to pack by stopping in Pomabamba near Jancapampa. This small town has some simple restaurants and shops to get food you can cook on the trail. But don't expect any processed snacks or food that packs as well as what you will find in Huaraz. I always prepare for the worst when it comes to food. Eleven days' worth of food was stuffed in my pack and was a significant weight for the first few days. I'd recommend planning on having enough food for the whole time and not relying on a resupply.

Permits and Reservations

Permits are required for entrance into the Huascarán National Park. There is a control point at Cashapampa where you may purchase a pass, but instead I recommend purchasing your pass ahead of time at the National Park office in Huaraz (-9.532854, -77.530088). This way, you won't deal with any uncertainty of their availability or rangers that cannot sell you a ticket, etc. Entrance rates for tourists are 30 soles for one day, 60 soles for two to three days, or 150 soles for 4-30 days. You will need the 4-30 day pass if you intend to complete the Alpamayo Circuit. This ticket also covers some of the fees if you choose to hike to Laguna Parón or Laguna 69. FYI there is a separate ticket for the Santa Cruz Trek you can purchase if you only want to complete that trek. When you buy the ticket in Huaraz, you can specify the start date of the thirty-day period. It doesn't have to start on the day you buy it. It is most fortunate that these permits are easily attainable when you arrive in Huaraz. Advanced planning is not required.

Item	**Cost (Soles)**
Huaraz to Caraz Collectivo	7 per person
Caraz Hostel	30
Caraz to Cashapampa Collectivo	15 per person
Huascarán 30 Day Permit	150 per person

Alpamayo Circuit Trail Map

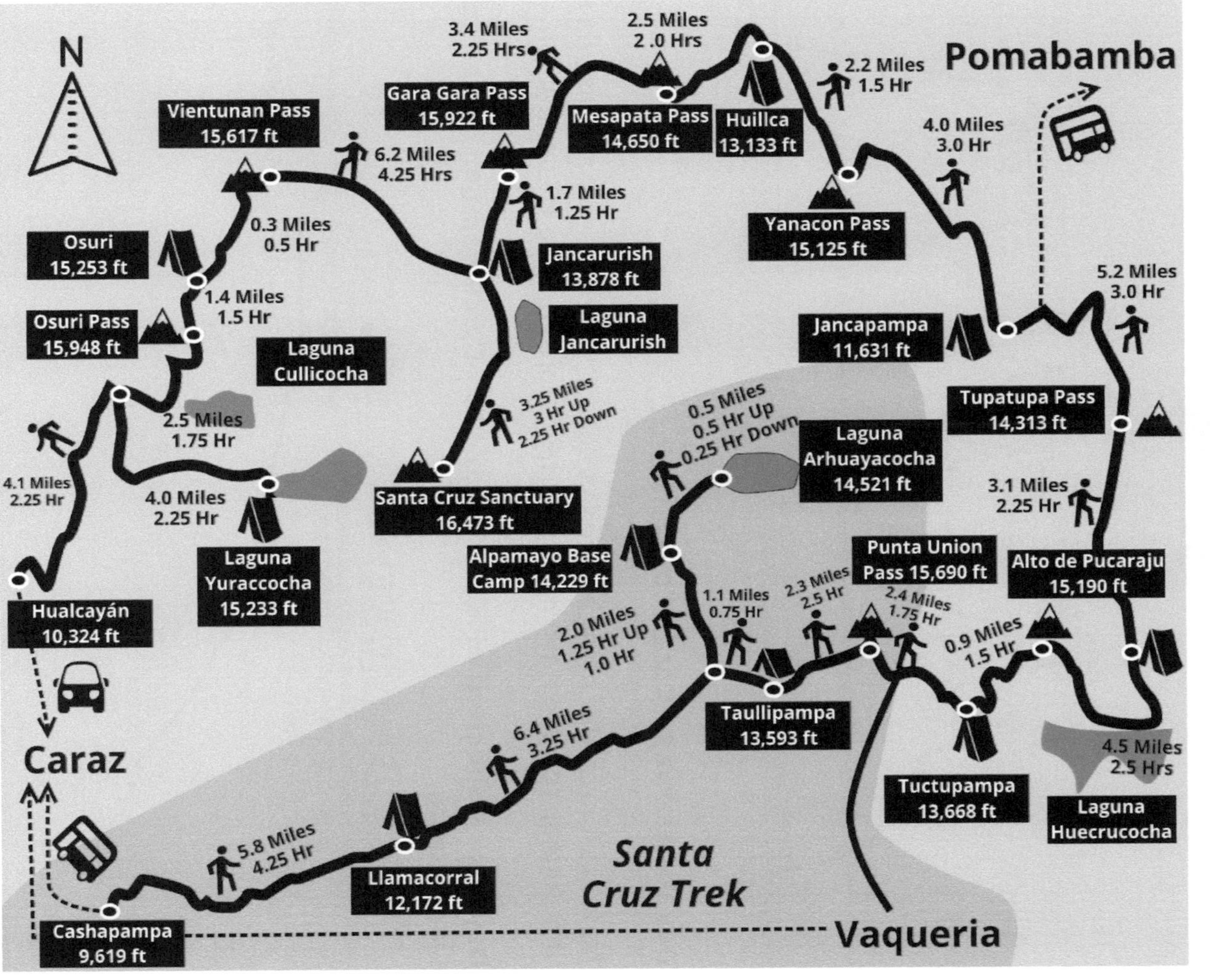

Recommended Itinerary – 11 Days Chasing Solitude

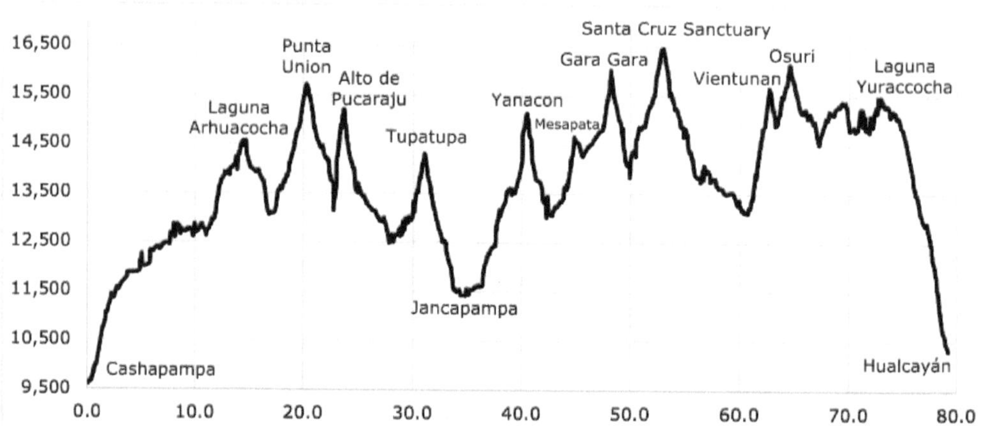

Day 0: Huaraz to Caraz Collectivo

Travel to Caraz the night before instead of very early on the first day of trekking. You will have more energy before tackling this marathon.

Day 1: Collectivo From Caraz to Cashapampa. Hike to Llamacorral

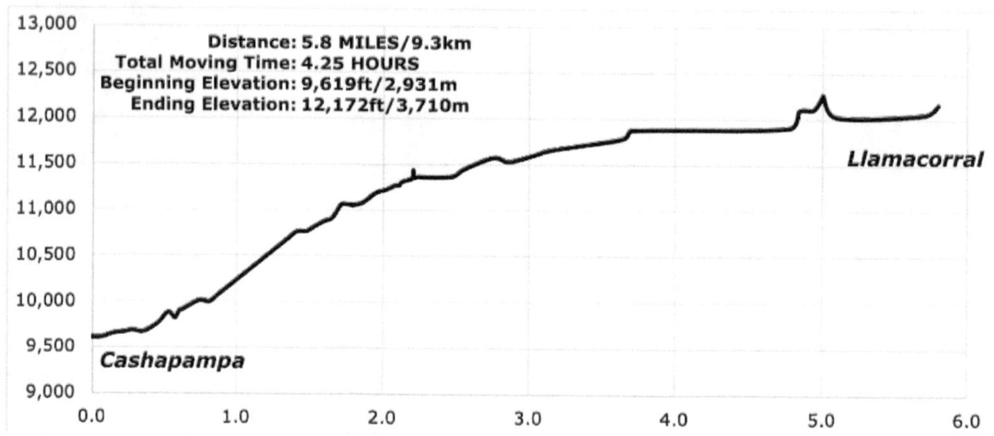

Make your way to the collectivo stand in Caraz and find a driver who will be stopping in Cashapampa. When you look at a map, Caraz and Cashapampa appear to be only a few miles away. Only real life will illustrate how this short distance is separated by endless winding dirt roads climbing up the sides of mountains. It takes about ninety minutes to get from Caraz to Cashapampa. Keep your eye out for the trailhead "Ruta De Trekking Santa Cruz" on your right side as you drive through the tiny village.

Trailhead Sign in Cashapampa (-8.95695, -77.77734)

From the trailhead, follow the small dirt path uphill until you reach the ranger station (-8.95398, -77.77545) to present your Huascarán National Park pass. Even at this relatively low elevation, the 2,500 feet of elevation to gain on the first day is challenging. The trail follows the valley and river uphill for the entire 5.8 miles to Llamacorral. Water is accessible throughout the whole first day of trekking. The first half of the hike up offers the steepest terrain, and then the gradient begins to level out as you approach the campground. It is evident how the flora of the trail changes as you ascend to over 12,000 feet. Bugs that tested your patience at the beginning of the day disappear. Lush trees are replaced with shorter shrubs and plants. The whole section is only 4.25 hours, so you should make it to camp with plenty of time to prepare for a much longer Day 2.

Llamacorral Campground: 12,172 feet

Day 2: Llamacorral to Taullipampa With a Side Trip to Alpamayo Base Camp and Laguna Arhuacocha

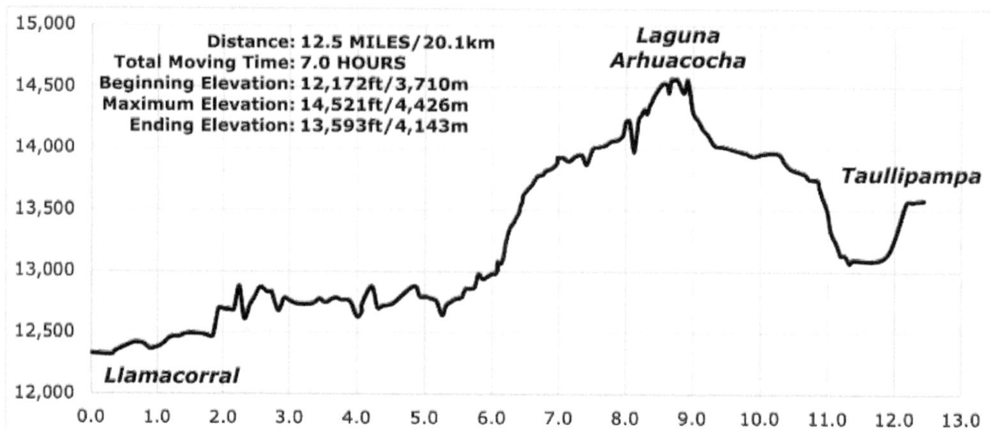

After a challenging warmup hike on Day 1, Day 2 is even more robust and offers the first views of Mt. Alpamayo and other giant ice-capped peaks. The entire day's trek overlaps with the Santa Cruz Trek, so you will see neighboring tour groups tackling this day either in the same direction or reverse. It is a beautiful hike up through the valley with a straightforward trail leading first to the massive Jatuncocha Lake. The trail remains mostly level as you continue northeast from Jatuncocha, leading you across a surprisingly arid landscape. Choose your path as you traverse across this spine of desert-like terrain until you reach the Jatunquisuar Campground (-8.91554, -77.62315). From Llamacorral to Jatunquisuar will require between 3 and 3.5 hours of moving time.

Jatunquisuar marks the bottom of the optional Alpamayo Basecamp day hike. Mt. Alpamayo has two basecamps for mountaineers aiming to reach the summit, one on the southern face and one on the northern front. Beyond the southern Alpamayo Basecamp is the stunning Laguna Arhuaycocha, a glacier lake hidden away and towered over by Mt. Rinrihirca and Puchahirca Sur. This side trip will add another three hours of moving time to the day. I highly recommend adding this side trip for the incredible views at Laguna Arhuaycocha. Not many trekkers make this excursion, so it will also provide an opportunity to escape the crowds of the Santa Cruz Trek.

Trail Leading to Alpamayo Basecamp

Shed off your large pack and exchange for a daypack. I felt comfortable tucking away my backpack in the woods nearby for the few hours I would be gone. The trail from Jatunquisuar heads north with a vigorous series of switchbacks rapidly gaining a healthy amount of elevation. If you turn around towards the direction from which you came, you will see the majestic Mt. Artesonraju. On the other side of that mountain is Laguna Parón! It will take 1.25 hours of hiking uphill to arrive at the Alpamayo Basecamp from Jatunquisuar. When I arrived at the Alpamayo Basecamp, the exhaustion hit me hard, and I seriously considered skipping the additional thirty-minute hike up to the Laguna Arhuaycocha. What a grand mistake that would have been. The extra 300 feet of elevation gain to the lake pushed my endurance and mental fortitude. Every step was worth getting to spend time with this hidden gem. Laguna Arhuaycocha was spectacular. Push yourself up to this spot, enjoy a nice lunch, and then descend back to Jatunquisuar for the final segment of the day.

Laguna Arhuaycocha: 14,521 feet

The final section of the day includes one more burst of uphill climbing to the Taullipampa Campground. Even though it will take less than an hour, do not underestimate it. After a full day of hiking, this last bit greatly challenged me. It was a significant relief unloading my pack, setting up camp, and taking in all of the beauty surrounding Taullipampa.

Taullipampa Campground: 13,593 feet

Day 3: Taullipampa to Tuctupampa via Punta Union Pass

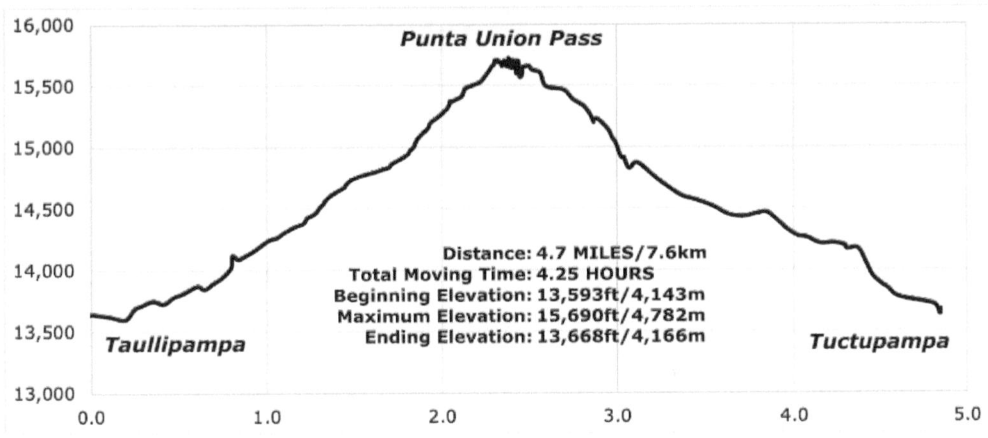

Both in terms of distance and moving time, this will be the shortest day of the Alpamayo Circuit. The Punta Union Pass is the highlight of the Santa Cruz Trek, reaching 15,690 feet and offering stunning 360-degree views. Only after putting in a solid 2.5 hours of strenuous uphill climbing from Taullipampa will you receive the gift of this spectacular vantage point. The trail reaching the pass is clear to follow to the summit. Along the hike up, views of Mt. Taulliraju and Laguna Taullicocha reveal themselves making the hard ascent up to the pass even more exhilarating. From 15,690 feet, you can see all of the hiking done on Day 2 and look into the future where you will be during the high point the next day. Since this was a short day, there was ample time to truly soak in every inch of this view and etch it into memory forever.

Punta Union Pass: 15,690 feet

Once you are ready for the final descent of the day, hike down the eastern face towards Laguna Morococha. The slope is very steep, making those trekking poles quite useful. After 1.5-2 hours of hiking from the pass, be on the sharp lookout for a break off the trail downhill to the left from the main trail (-8.92122, -77.5639). This fork in the path is not marked at all and can easily be missed. After you turn left, the overlap that the Alpamayo Circuit has with the Santa Cruz trek is over. From the fork onward represents the start of more remote and wild sections. Tuctupampa Campground is located at the base of the valley and a bit further south than where the trail feeds into the valley, no more than twenty minutes from the fork. Look for the human-made circular stone structure marking the site (-8.92357, -77.55871).

Day 4: Tuctupampa to Huecrucocha Area via Alto de Pucaraju

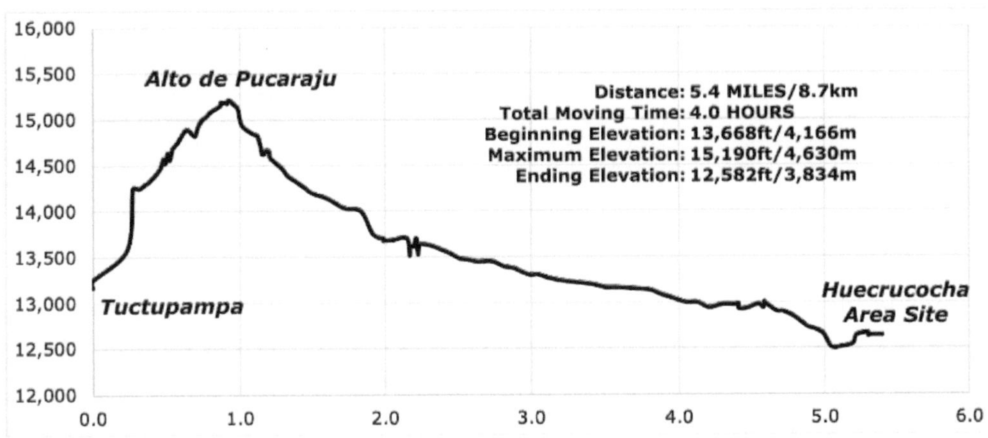

Gone are the easy-to-follow trails. Day 4 is the first navigationally challenging portion of the Alpamayo Circuit. The freedom to create your own path can be a fun new experience for some used to highway trails. For others, the mental strain of deciding where to take your feet and dealing with all the uncertainty of where you should be going can be too much. Luckily, the path up to the Alto de Pucaraju is not hard to find. The trail heads uphill to the northeast from Tuctupampa. Find the trail sign just north of the campsite before crossing the river to the east. The ninety-minute climb up the Alto de Pucaraju is not quite as hard as the ascent to Punta Union, but by Day 4, it will still be a good challenge. From the summit of the pass, there is an excellent view of the Punta Union pass towards the west, Mt. Taulliraju to the north, and a vast valley continuing down to the east.

Alto de Pucaraju - 15,190 feet

Enjoy the view for an hour before descending the east face of the pass. There are a series of trails you can follow down to the valley floor. Once they reach the valley floor, the trails disappear. Even in the dry season, the ground was extremely saturated. Hiking without a path across this labyrinth of streams made it challenging to keep boots dry. Keep following the left side of the river that carves through the valley until the trail leading to Huecrucocha becomes more pronounced. You should aim for the trail that leads to the northern shore of the large lake. The trail eventually descends to the lake level as you continue east. Take a rest when you reach the far northeast side of the lake. However, I would not swim in this lake because it is used as a fishery for the locals. My initial plan was to camp next to the lake but I was unable to find suitable ground for a tent. In search of a better campsite, I continued further along the trail into the next valley. The trail continues east with a large river outflowing from Huecrucocha on your left. Descend to the valley floor and find the small log bridge that crosses the river heading northwest. Much of the land in this valley is saturated and not fit for a tent. I was able to find a great dry spot to set up my tent high on the east side of the river, about 0.3 miles up the valley from the river crossing (-8.91928, -77.51168).

Camping Area in Valley Passed Laguna Huecrucocha

Day 5: Huecrucocha Area to Jancapampa via Tupatupa Pass

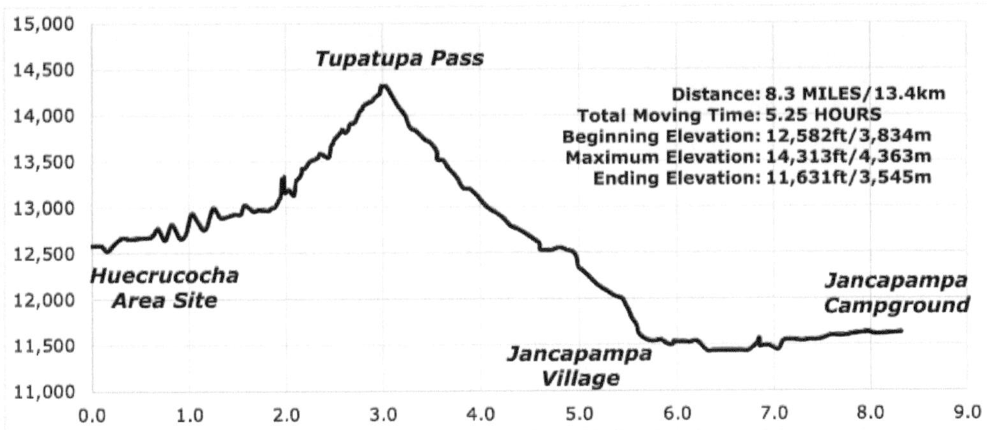

The navigational challenges continue on Day 5 as you try to find the way up to the Tupatupa Pass. Follow the valley uphill on the left side while trying to keep your boots dry in this saturated ground. There are no trail signs nor human-made markers of any kind, indicating where in the valley you should cross to the east side of the river and hike north uphill to the pass. The icon that you should be keeping your eye out for on the north side of the valley is an isolated dry peak with a skinny plateaued top. When you find that peak, you will hike uphill with that peak on your right side. Forging a path uphill through the thick brush was tough. If you are using GPS to guide you, aim for a small unnamed lake at (-8.88807, -77.52266). Trails become more pronounced the higher you climb. Once you find this lake, the path is obvious to the summit Tupatupa Pass. This pass might be the least visually impressive of the circuit, but there are still some great views of the surrounding peaks and valleys.

Approximate Trail to Tupatupa Pass. Stay Left of the Circled Plateau Peak

The summit of the Tupatupa Pass will be an optimal break for lunch before heading down to Jancapampa. There is a clear trail hiking downhill north to the valley of Jancapampa. As you approach the village, you'll see private farmland with tons of animals grazing and beautiful flora with Mt. Pucajirca in the background. There is no preferable way down; keep walking downhill until you either reach the Jancapampa village or the valley floor. There is a dirt road that travels west on the south side of the valley.

Descent into the valley neighboring Jancapampa

If you are craving beer or something sweet, walk into the village along the dirt road and find the building with a "Se Vende" sign posted on the outside. After five days of hiking, a couple of candy bars and a bottle of coke was heaven. There is a collectivo that picks up right near this shop at the river bridge and goes to the neighboring Pomabamba village if you want access to more food options or want to call it quits and get a long bus ride back to Huaraz.

Small Shop with Candy, Soda, and Beer For Sale

Once you have gotten a quick snack, hike west on the dirt road across the valley to the very end. From the terminus of the dirt road, continue hiking west for about 0.6 miles and slowly angle your path north. Again, there are no trail signs or human-made markers indicating where the camping area is. Cross the river to the north side until you find the suitable land for a tent (-8.85178, -77.55051). There are no official markings for the campsite, but some clear flat spots located a bit uphill from the river will provide adequate shelter for the night.

Day 6: Jancapampa to Huillca via Yanacon Pass

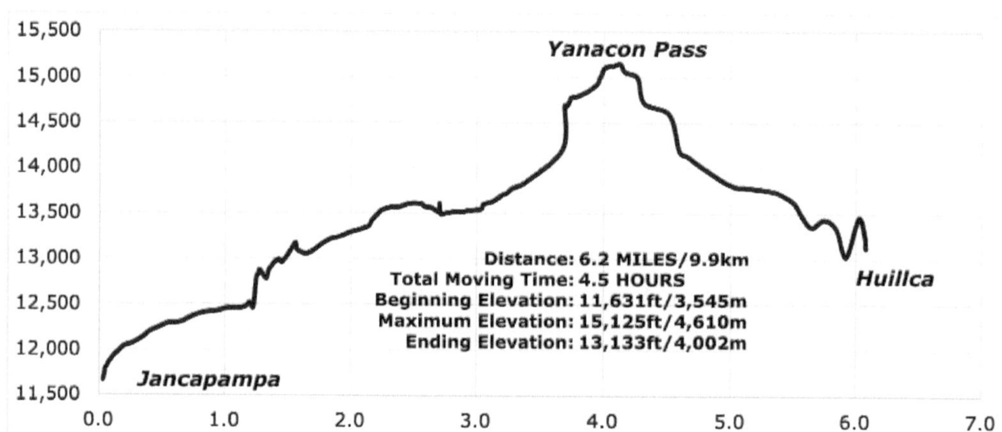

Day 6 is the third and last day of navigation difficulties on the Alpamayo Circuit. With more than 3,500 feet of elevation gain, this is also the most physically brutal day. Finding the Yanacon Pass without a guide is similarly challenging as the previous two days, but with much more elevation gain. The first half of the hike from the Jancapampa Campground up to the Yanacon Pass is easy to follow with steady uphill. The trail starts with a steep climb with the river flowing downhill on the left until it crosses the river to the west side, heading north. After about an hour of hiking, the narrow path widens into a large opening with a few crumbling stone structures. Cross the small stream (-8.83912, -77.55592) heading north and then turn west and find the path leading uphill. The next 2.8 miles up to the summit of the Yanacon Pass include a wide valley without a clear trail heading uphill and a bit of a scramble, finally leading to the summit. Follow any of the herding trails up near the end of the valley traveling west. Begin the uphill ascent from the floor before the valley ends on the left (south) side with the dark brown rock wall on your left side. Keep hiking uphill on the south side of the valley until the trail becomes more pronounced and starts to curve to the right (north). The final section leading up to the pass finally provides a well-trodden path.

Approximate Trail to Yanacon Pass

All of the hard work reaching the Yanacon Pass is rewarded with stunning panoramic views. Enjoy a highly deserved break before making the final push of the day descending to Huillca. The northern side of the pass is relatively easy to follow compared to the southern ascent. It only takes ninety minutes to make the descent to Huillca. Hike past the small property at the base of the valley, curve left, and find a wide flat area next to the river to set up camp (-8.80666, -77.60882).

Huillca Campground: 13,133 feet

Day 7: Huillca to Jancarurish via Mesapata and Gara Gara Passes

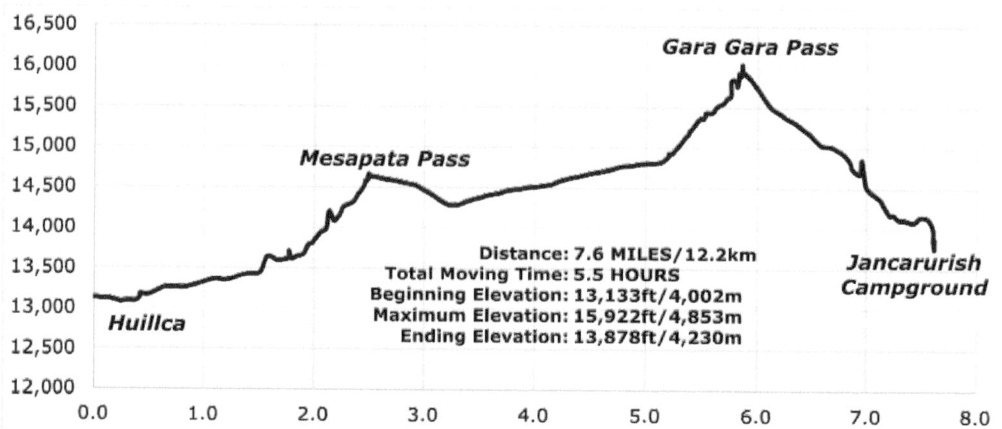

Two challenging passes separate the start and finish line on the seventh day of the Alpamayo Circuit. From Huillca, hike 1/3 mile northwest and cross to the western side of the major river splitting the adjacent valley to the southwest. After crossing the river, make a sharp left turn hike uphill southwest until finding what feels like a broad highway dirt trail. Follow this wide trail up until finding a fork (-8.81158, -77.62496). Turn right off the main path, slowly gaining elevation. Fight gravity trying to keep you low and hike uphill on the high right side. Half of a mile after the fork, pivot your trajectory northwest and follow the trails uphill to the first pass of the day, Mesapata Pass (-8.81058, -77.63568).

Mesapata Pass Looking South: 14,650 feet

Don't take too long resting at the Mesapata Pass because there is an even harder one coming up. The trail stays high as it descends west until losing elevation to the bottom. Cross the valley to the northern side and find the path that traces the direction of the pass a bit elevated from the floor. The trail is easy to follow for the next few miles leading to the base of the Gara Gara Pass. It is a steep climb to bank this pass just under 16,000 feet. After three days of challenging navigation, it will be a relief to have an easy to follow path reaching the Gara Gara Pass despite it being a significant physical test.

Gara Gara Pass: 15,922 feet

The views from Gara Gara are among the best anywhere on the Alpamayo Circuit. At this high vantage point are some of the first sights of Mt. Santa Cruz and the massive Laguna Jancarurish. Getting to camp from the pass only takes an additional 1.25 hours, so depending on how early you arrive at Gara Gara, you can potentially afford to enjoy a significant break at the top of this vista. After soaking in this spectacular lookout, follow the trail almost 2,000 feet downhill. At the bottom of the valley, cross the river bridge, turn right (west) away from the direction of the lake and walk 500 feet where you will find the Jancarurish Campground (-8.84621, -77.68166). If you do not plan on completing the optional Day 8 hike up to the Santa Cruz Sanctuary, hike up west for a stellar view of Laguna Jancarurish before crawling into the tent.

Jancarurish Campground with Mt. Alpamayo in Background: 13,878 feet

Day 8: Optional Day Hike to Santa Cruz Sanctuary

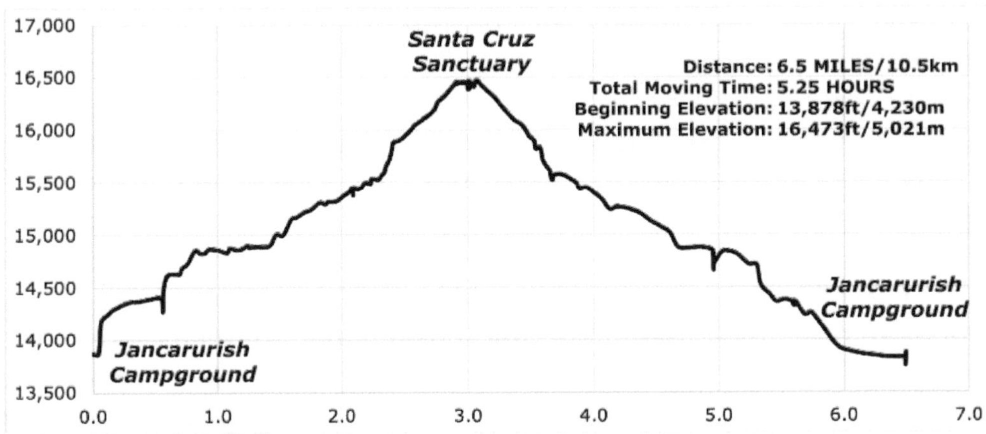

There are two options to extend the Alpamayo Circuit beyond the loop. The first day hike opportunity up to the Santa Cruz Sanctuary should not be missed. Like every hike throughout the Cordillera Blanca, spectacular views are rewarded to climbers willing to push through strenuous and unforgiving ascents. Most hikers I encountered along the way only climbed high enough for pictures of the beautiful Laguna Jancarurish and skipped the hard part: getting up to the sanctuary. Unless you have time constraints or other unforeseen factors accelerating your need to exit the circuit, add this beautiful hike to the plan.

Leave your gear at Jancarurish Campground at your own risk. A guide sharing the campground mentioned that there had been cases of theft at this spot in the past. My gear was fine left alone for the day, but you may opt to pack up camp and take it with you or find a safe place to hide it while you are out hiking for the day.

Uphill, south of the campground, is the trail leading southeast from Jancarurish Campground up to Laguna Jancarurish. You will hike 0.6 miles through some short trees and bushes until reaching a river crossing directly below the sharp uphill. From the river crossing, you can elect to stay low and continue hiking south, or you can climb uphill and walk south along the rim of the basin overlooking Laguna Jancarurish. The uphill climb is worth it for the fantastic views of the lake. *Be cautious hiking along the edge as there is an unforgiving descent hundreds of feet down to the lake.* After hiking south 0.3 miles, or almost halfway around the lake, the trail angles back downhill to rejoin the main trail. The trail climbs uphill significantly past a tranquil waterfall until you reach the Alpamayo North Basecamp (-8.86346, -77.67982). After the basecamp, continue southwest along the valley floor. Do not follow the path that goes uphill southeast from the basecamp as this is the way mountaineers utilize for summits to Alpamayo. This area is particularly saturated and lacking a distinct footpath until you reach the river crossing (-8.86746, -77.68238). There is no bridge to look for, but at this point, the other side is an easy rock jump across. *Do not hike any further south than this point before you cross the river to the western side as the gap becomes impossible to traverse.*

Somehow, there are more cairns marking the next section of the path than will be found throughout the entire Alpamayo Circuit. Keep following the path along the valley. The rocks begin to get larger the further you travel southwest from the river crossing. It is about a mile in between the river crossing and the bottom of the steep climb leading up to the moraine overlooking a huge unnamed lake (-8.87848, -77.69063). You will find a few abandoned stone structures close to this waypoint as well.

Steep Basin Leading to Santa Cruz Sanctuary

Hike along the path leading to the summit of the basin. Do not be fooled into thinking that the top of the basin is the finish line. From the top of the basin, continue west 0.5 miles until you reach a large rock shelf marked by a myriad of cairns indicating the summit of the Santa Cruz Sanctuary (-8.88093, -77.69777). The views all around from this vista are enchanting and are the ultimate setting for a significant lunch break. Keep your eye out for glacial ice cracking off the Santa Cruz mountain towering over the viewpoint.

Santa Cruz Sanctuary: 16,473 feet

At 16,473 feet, the Santa Cruz Sanctuary is the highest point anywhere along the Alpamayo Circuit. The 2,600 feet of elevation gain required to reach it is exhausting, and by Day 8, what might have been routine on fresh legs will feel more strenuous. Three hours of moving time will earn you complete views of the impressive mountain ranges and glacial lakes that scatter the landscape. The return trip will take 45 minutes less than the ascent, but still require commensurate time to maneuver through the saturated terrain leading to the Alpamayo North Basecamp.

Day 9: Jancarurish to Osuri via Vientunan Pass

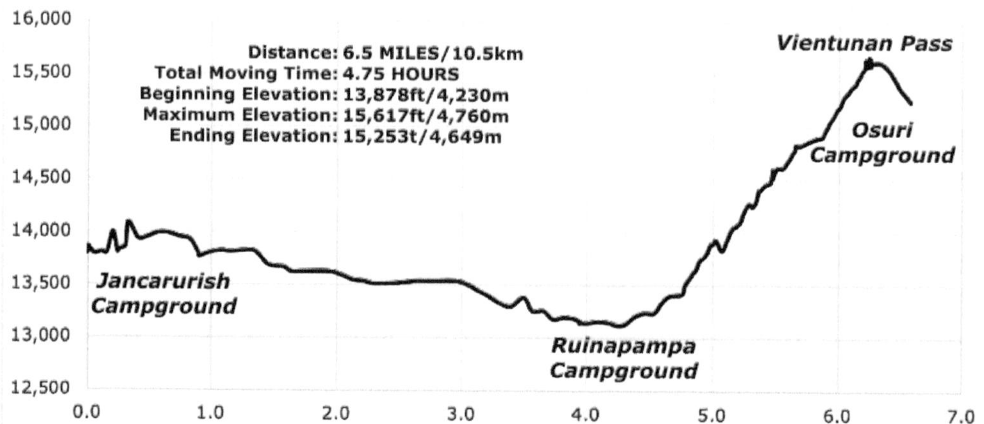

Day 9 has a bit of a different feel than most days because it starts with a descent and ends with a tough upward climb. Easy to follow trails will be a welcome change compared to much of the trekking over the past five days. Depart Jancarurish Campground and find the same path leading to Laguna Jancarurish but turn west towards Ruinapampa. The trail maintains elevation for the most part until lowering near the valley floor. The first waypoint to aim for is a small river crossing (-8.83705, -77.7023). After two hours of beautiful trekking with a downhill gradient, you can take a break at the Ruinapampa Campground along the river (-8.82870, -77.73323). The morning hike to Ruinapampa brings you down 700 feet to 13,163 feet and is just a warmup for the beast of an ascent to finish the day.

From Ruinapampa to the summit of Vientunan Pass is a seemingly endless series of switchbacks climbing almost 2,500 feet. By Day 9, every stretch feels like another mile under your feet. On a positive note, this climb has a rare, visible trail that requires no GPS or navigational effort. It takes about 2.5 hours to reach the top of the pass from Ruinapampa and requires a lot of determination and hard work. At the summit, enjoy the view for as long as you wish because only thirty minutes of hiking remain.

Vientunan Pass: 15,617 feet

There are two different sites known as "Osuri" that you have the choice between. The first site, which I camped at, is the smaller of the two and is closest to the Vientunan Pass (-8.84565, -77.74929). There is a small stream to fill up water. I shared this spot with a tour group, so it was a bit cramped, but there was adequate space for six to eight tents. If this campground is full, continue five minutes further down to the larger, official Osuri Campground that has a more extensive flat ground (-8.84604, -77.75233). Enjoy camping at the highest campsite throughout the Alpamayo Circuit.

Day 10: Osuri to Laguna Yuraccocha via Osuri Pass

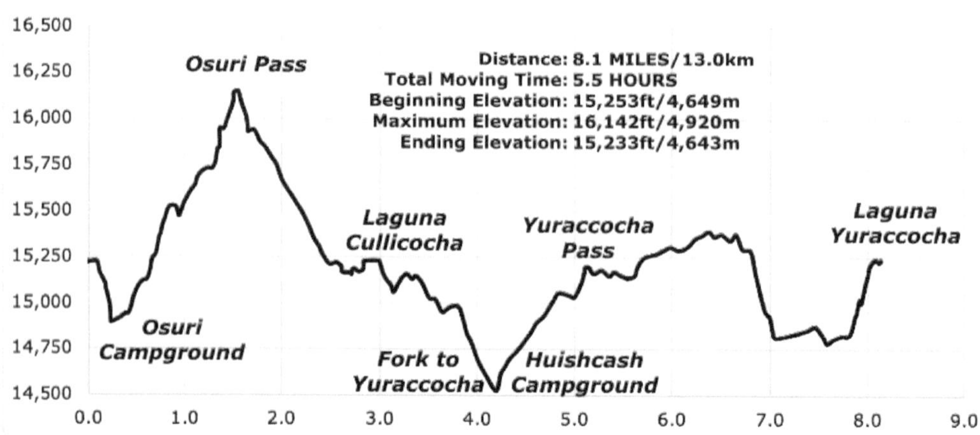

The penultimate day of the Alpamayo Circuit includes fantastic alpine views, a chance to fully immerse yourself into a glacial lake, and a roller coast hike with ups and downs the entire way. There are two options to consider for where Day 10 will conclude. Laguna Yuraccocha is an optional add-on destination. My itinerary had me camping at Yuraccocha on Day 10 and then returning to the main trail on the morning of Day 11. If you are looking to reduce the mileage, it is possible to skip Yuraccocha and camp instead at Huishcash. The beauty of not having reservations for campsites is that you can make spontaneous decisions based on how you are physically feeling at this point deep within the circuit.

If you stayed at the smaller Osuri Campground site, start the day by hiking down to the main Osuri Campground and get ready for a tough uphill climb. It is easy to follow the trail to the Osuri Pass, but several false summits will make this hike mentally and physically demanding. When you reach the top of the pass at 15,948 feet, the views are not impressive. I was fortunate to learn from another guide that the worthwhile lookout is only a ten-minute scramble up the rocks heading east from the pass (-8.85838, -77.75341). The views from this unofficial vista are breathtaking with Laguna Cullicocha and the Santa Cruz mountain towering in the background.

This experience was a perfect reminder of the benefits of making connections and learning from other people you meet along the trail. I am sure that if I hadn't started a conversation with this guide, I would have reached the pass and continued down without knowing that an unforgettable view was only ten minutes higher off the trail. Always assume that travelers around you know something valuable. Talk and share insights with those that you meet; you will reap in the rewards.

Osuri Viewpoint (Not the Pass!): 16,142 feet

Continue from the Osuri Viewpoint and Pass down about a mile to Laguna Cullicocha. On a perfect sunny day, this freezing lake was precisely the outdoor shower that my body needed after seemingly countless days on the trail. The path snakes around the edge of the valley following the river downhill. It is effortless to follow the trail about an hour from Cullicocha to the fork leading either to Laguna Yuraccocha or down to Huishcash and eventually the end of the circuit at Hualcayán (-8.86672, -77.77397). Look for a concrete block that used to hold a sign marking the fork. If you want the day to be over, you should be able to see Huishcash Campground from the fork and hike five minutes downhill to conclude the day.

I highly recommend continuing to Laguna Yuraccocha because it will give you one last night of camping in paradise. Complete solitude at this dazzling oasis is worth the extra 4.0 miles it adds to the day. From the fork, the trail heads south, gaining elevation quickly until reaching the Yuraccocha Pass (-8.88054, -77.77307). This is more of a mock pass because there is more uphill after. The next 1.5 miles is a roller coaster going up and down, heading east high along the valley. Just before Mile 7, the trail loses a steep amount of elevation that you must stubbornly gain again before reaching the laguna. Before the final push up to the lake is a flat spot with a few abandoned stone structures. Hike uphill and a bit to the right until you find the small reservoir immediately south of the lake. Walk along the north side of the pool over the concrete duct, and out of nowhere, the entire Laguna Yuraccocha will reveal itself in all its splendor. There is limited adequate tent space along the lake. I found my patch of flat ground to the right (south) of the concrete duct controlling water out of the lake (-8.88431, -77.73598).

Approximate Trail Leading to Laguna Yuraccocha

Another note worth mentioning: if you are pressed for time, it would be possible to skip Yuraccocha and hike from Osuri to the exit of the Alpamayo Circuit in Hualcayán. However, I do not recommend doing this because arriving in Hualcayán late in the day will make getting a ride back to Caraz more difficult.

Day 11: Laguna Yuraccocha to Hualcayán. Ride back to Caraz.

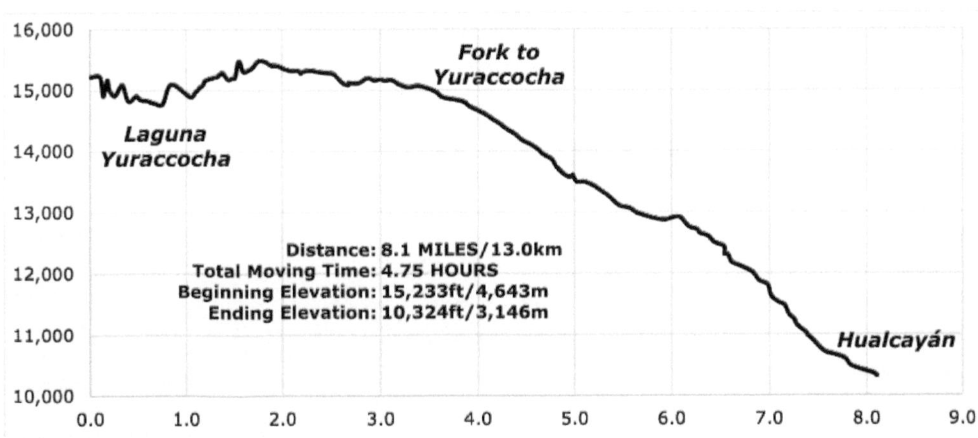

The final day of the Alpamayo Circuit is highlighted by almost 5,000 feet of elevation loss down to the village of Hualcayán. Start the day very early because the sooner you arrive at Hualcayán, the easier it will be to find a ride back to Caraz. Your goal should be to arrive by 14:00 at the latest. Return to the main trail from Yuraccocha following the same path as yesterday over the Yuraccocha Pass. From the fork, turn left and descend towards Huishcash. Descending to Hualcayán takes 2.25 hours from the fork and will be a punishment on the knees for those who did not pack trekking poles. Endless switchbacks are the only thing in between you and the finish line.

After a grueling descent, you will better understand why I recommend starting in Cashapampa as opposed to Hualcayán. For how hard of a hike down it is, hiking uphill the opposite direction with a full pack would be another level of difficulty. The village of Hualcayán is tiny, with a few shops but no restaurants or lodging. There are three options for returning to Caraz. Ideally, you will find a tour group that has a private bus heading to Caraz and solicit a ride. If that fails, the next best option is to find a private taxi ride or collectivo from the village square. The unfortunate truth about these small villages is that transportation is unreliable. A risk of hiking this route is that there are no guaranteed private or public transportation methods to get back to Caraz. The worst-case scenario is walking about four hours along the dirt road back to Cashapampa, where there are more regular transports to Caraz.

Laguna Parón

Huascarán National Park offers enough trails to occupy trekkers until their knees fall off. There are endless opportunities for day hikes and multi-day hikes. Shorter hikes can be a useful bridge in between longer extended circuits such as the Huayhuash Circuit and the Alpamayo Circuit. As you walk throughout the city of Huaraz, you will see a horde of trekking companies offering excursions to several of the park's highlights. A day trip to the exquisite Laguna Parón is a popular option offered by many companies. This massive turquoise lake deserves to make your trip's itinerary because the views are spectacular, and the camping is world-class. The question you will face isn't whether or not you should visit Laguna Parón. It is how you will get there and if you will visit independently or with a guided service.

If there is a way for me to hike independently, I am going to take it. Even though the logistics can often be more frustrating, the satisfaction I feel knowing I earned a view is worth it. Choosing to visit Laguna Parón independently has distinct pros and cons. Guided tours leave Huaraz early in the morning, drive several hours up winding dirt roads past the village of Parón to the actual water's edge of Laguna Parón, offer you an hour or so to walk around, and then drive you back into town. The tour is convenient and takes a lot of the challenging logistics out of your hands. The main disadvantage of joining a guided tour is the limited time available to explore and enjoy the views at Laguna Parón. If you only have one day to visit the lake, it makes much more sense to go with the tour. Choosing the independent route allows you the chance to camp overnight and take in the full experience.

The challenge of transportation is the biggest puzzle to solve when visiting the lake. Getting to the Laguna Parón isn't too complicated even though there aren't any direct collectivos or public bus options. The best alternative for getting to Laguna Parón without a tour group is hiring a taxi from Caraz to the village of Parón for 15 soles. Once in the village you have two options. You can hike the 2,800 feet of elevation that separates the village of Parón and Laguna Parón or you can hire a taxi for 100 soles. The taxi will save you from a 2.5 hour hike. At the same time, you end up with a more expensive visit. If you are budget conscious, hike the way up to Laguna Parón from the Parón village.

The real logistical challenge of visiting Laguna Parón independently is transportation back to Caraz at the end. There are no collectivos that you can count on to take you back to Caraz from this remote village or from the actual lake. Taxis will most likely not be available for hire. My recommended strategy is to arrange for the same taxi driver to return to the drop off point at an agreed upon time the next day. Offer to pay the driver a portion of the return fare in advance but leave enough unpaid to still incentivize him or her to keep their word. This is certainly not a foolproof plan, as I personally experienced. The first backup plan to return on your own to Caraz or Huaraz is to hitch a ride with a tour bus. This turned out to work out fine for me. The worst case scenario is to hike the eight miles back to Huaraz.

Laguna Parón Trail Map

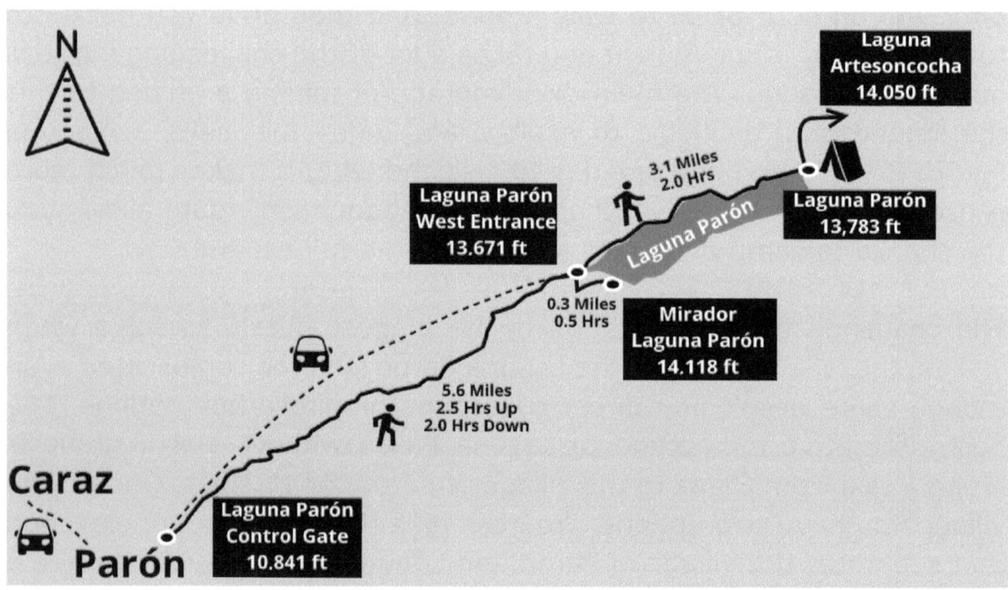

Recommended Itinerary – Laguna Parón

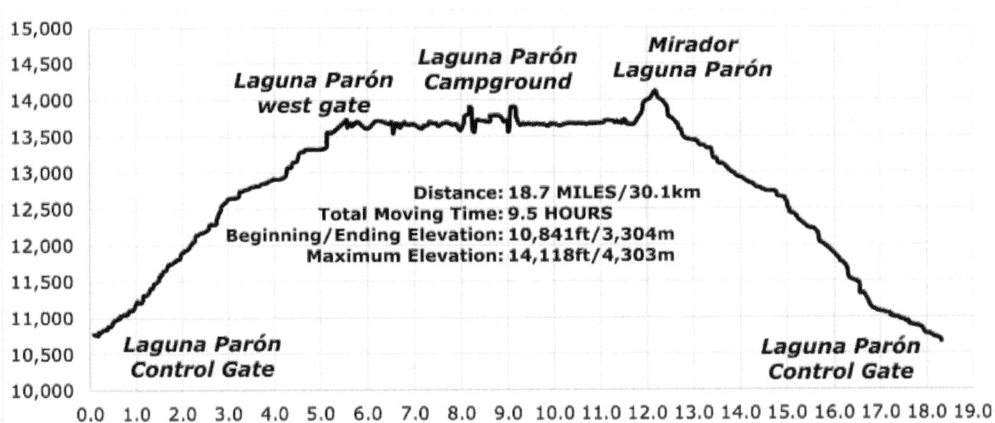

Depart Caraz first thing in the morning to arrive in the village of Parón no later than 10:00. Request that your taxi driver drops you off at the Laguna Parón Control Gate (-9.03843, -77.73244) just past the village. Here, an officer will check that you have a Huascarán National Park entrance ticket, and also sell you a minimal Laguna Parón specific entrance fee. The trail leading up to Laguna Parón meanders along the nearby river up the valley and frequently overlaps with the main dirt road. The majority of this 5.6 mile grind up 2,800 feet is well marked. When walking on the road, be observant for large tour buses that race up to the top with little regard to pedestrians. It takes a tough 2.5 hours of uphill climbing to reach the entrance of Laguna Parón.

After reaching the western edge of Laguna Parón, there are two options to consider. The first option is to walk up the southwestern ridgeline to the Laguna Parón Viewpoint (-9.00054, -77.68198). You need to take this hour long roundtrip at some point during your visit. The elevated view of the lake with all the soaring mountains is exquisite. For my visit, I didn't arrive at Laguna Parón until 13:00, and I still had a couple hours of hiking to get to camp. So, I elected to save the viewpoint for the second day.

The camping spots at Laguna Parón are located far on the opposite side of the lake from the main entrance. It is easy to underestimate this segment of the hike because you can see the destination the whole time. This creates a convincing illusion that you don't have far to go. The truth is that it takes a full two hours to hike 3.1 miles around the lake. The trail runs along the northern shore of Laguna Parón without much elevation gain or loss. Follow the trail east along the shoreline. After about 2.5 miles, the trail along the shoreline gets cut off, and you are forced to hike steep uphill on the left side (-8.98504, -77.65739). The trail used to simply continue along the shoreline, but fallen rocks now force hikers to hike above the shore to get to the eastern side of the lake. I was unable to find any officially marked campground on the eastern shore but found plenty of nice flat land to set up a tent (-8.9853, -77.65473).

The second day is simply the reverse of the first day. Pack up camp and retrace your steps back to the Laguna Parón entrance on the western side of the lake. If you did not get the opportunity to visit the Laguna Parón Viewpoint on the first day, make sure to do so before descending to the Parón village. Hiking downhill will save at least thirty minutes compared to the ascent. Returning to Caraz will be dependent on what arrangements you made with your taxi driver.

One flaw in this itinerary was not having enough time to hike up to Laguna Artesoncocha as I originally planned. This lake is further uphill about a mile from the eastern edge of Laguna Parón. A mixture of exhaustion and diminishing sunlight prevented me from reaching the lake on Day 1, and on the second day, the weather conditions did not warrant the climb up. If you want to include this hike into your Laguna Parón trip, either plan on an early morning wakeup on Day 2 to reach the lake, or better yet, plan on spending an extra day so you have plenty of time to explore. Hiking up to Laguna Artesoncocha and then getting back to Parón village would be a particularly long and challenging day that I was not prepared for. It would be possible to fit in the hike up to Laguna Artesoncocha on Day 1 if you paid for a ride all the way up to the lake instead of just to the village.

Laguna 69/Pisco Basecamp

Laguna 69 is the most popular day hike offered to visitors in the Huascarán National Park. With a catchy name that raises eyebrows, it deservedly attracts attention. The hike to Laguna 69 is frequently used as an acclimatizing trip for those preparing for more extensive treks like the Santa Cruz and Huayhuash Circuit. The lake is beautiful, and pictures of its divine turquoise waters are plastered on advertisements throughout Huaraz. Similar to the Laguna Parón hike, the most popular way to visit the lake is with a tour company as a day hike. A tour company is an excellent option for visitors with restricted time. If you have more flexibility, it is possible to extend the visit into a more fun and adventurous overnight by including a stay at the Pisco Basecamp/Refugio Peru. Trekkers who choose to hike independently of a tour guide are rewarded by the flexibility to hike at their own pace and a chance to beat the crowds to the lake.

Refugio Peru is one of many cabin lodges found throughout Huascarán National Park, offering relatively luxurious lodging opportunities. Most occupants of the Pisco Basecamp and Refugio Peru are mountaineers preparing for ascents to the summit of Mt. Pisco. Even if you do not have ambitions to summit this 18,871 ft giant, it is still a great place to hike to and enjoy the small luxuries such as hot cooked meals and a comfortable place to rest. Adding this overnight segment will provide you a more elevated and colorful experience compared to solely completing the day hike. Navigating is not a concern for any of the trip.

Laguna 69/Pisco Basecamp Trail Map

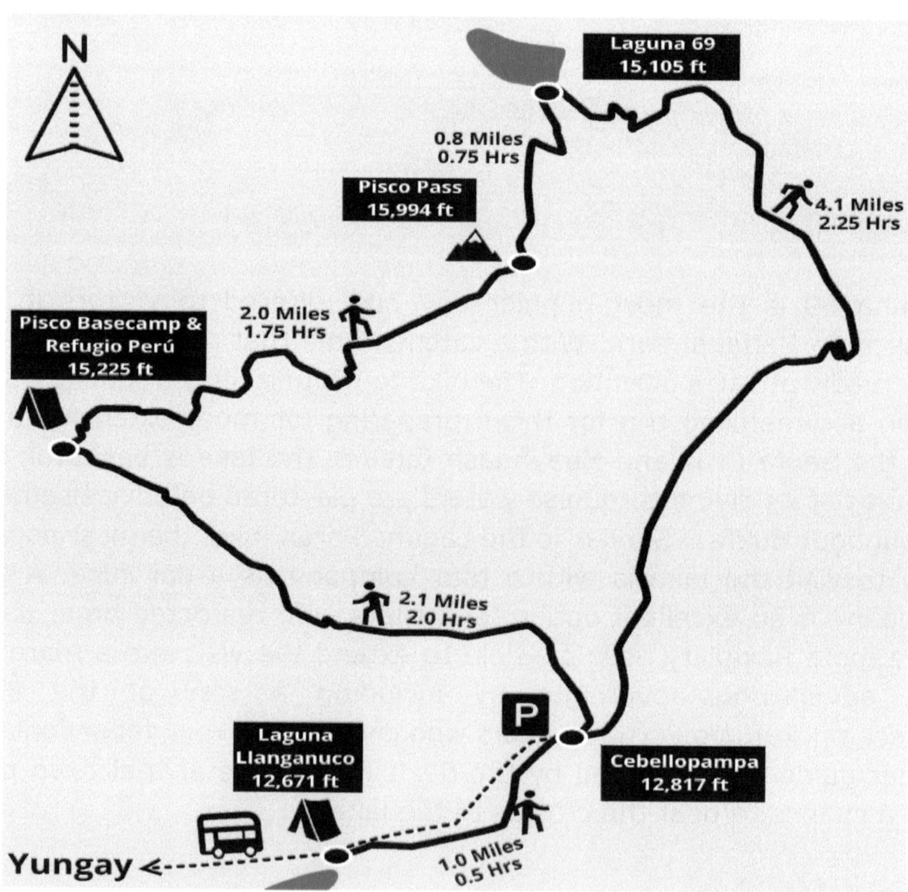

Recommended Itinerary - Pisco Basecamp+Laguna 69 Overnight

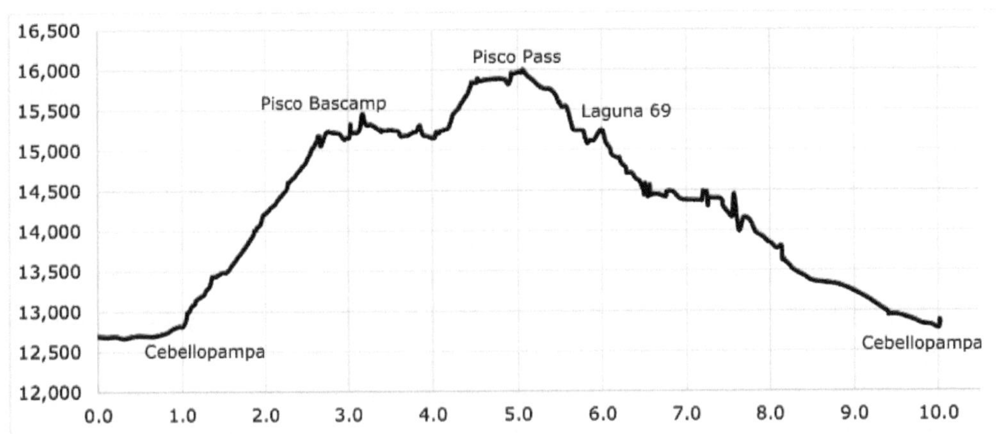

Day 1: Lake Llanganuco Campground to Pisco Basecamp

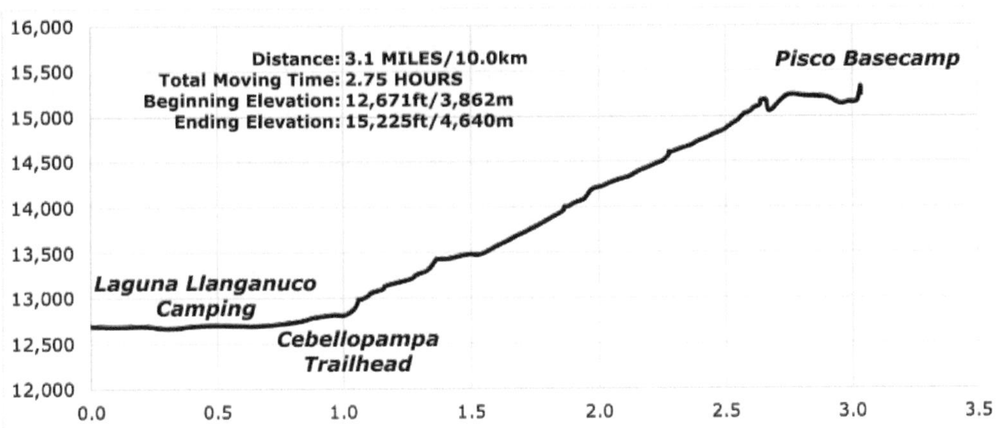

The trailhead for both the Laguna 69 day hike and the extended overnight version is Cebellopampa. This spot is located northeast along Route 106 from the town of Yungay. To get to Cebellopampa, first take the same collectivo that commutes between Huaraz and Caraz and get off at the Yungay bus terminal. There are tons of collectivos and private transportation options available there. To find the correct ride, ask the drivers for Laguna 69, Santa Cruz Trek, or Vaqueria village. Any collectivo going to Vaqueria, the trailhead for the popular Santa Cruz Trek, will be able to drop you off at the Cebellopampa trailhead. The driver I hired in Yungay offered to take me to the trailhead for 30 soles (~$9).

It takes an hour and a half to drive from Yungay up to the Cebellopampa trailhead. It is a pretty bland drive until reaching the stunning Llanganuco Lagunas. These giant lakes alone would be worth the visit. For reasons that were unclear to me, the driver would only go as far as the Llanganuco Campground located one mile west from the Cebellopampa trailhead. You should be able to get dropped off directly at the trailhead. After reaching the Cebellopampa trailhead, there is a clear trail marker indicating whether you want to go directly up to Laguna 69, or take the trail leading to Pisco Basecamp. Take the left fork heading towards Pisco Basecamp. A fully formed trail leads up 2,400 feet over just 2.1 miles to the Pisco Basecamp. The camping area is located downhill south from Refugio Peru. Even if you are not lodging at Refugio Peru, you can still visit the lodge and get some hot food and drink. The Refugio is also the best place to get water; they offer untreated cold water for free.

Refugio Peru: 15,225 feet

Day 2: Pisco Basecamp to Laguna 69, Exit Via Cebellopampa

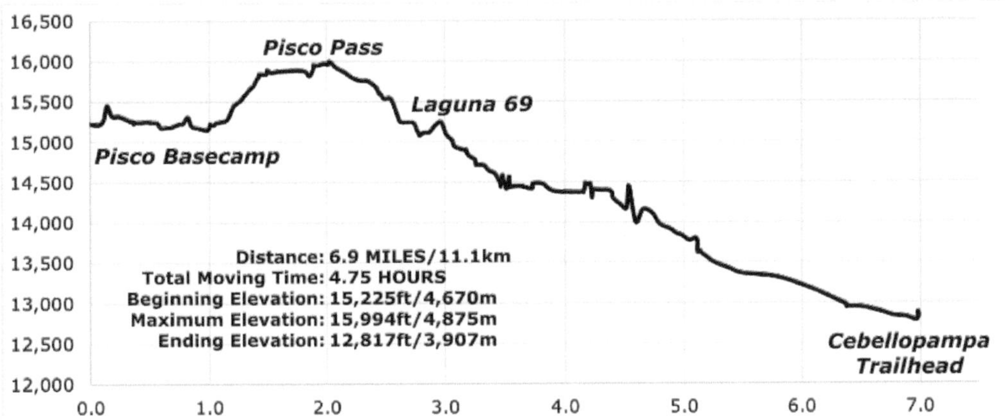

A significant benefit of hiking to Laguna 69 independently is the chance to enjoy the natural wonder before the day hikers arrive. The fastest climbers from the day trips will arrive at the lake by 09:00. I suggest arriving at the lake by at least 08:30 so that you get a half-hour of solitude before the swarm arrives. It takes between two and three hours to hike from the Pisco Basecamp. An early start will be worth those precious minutes of peace at this gem.

The trail begins at Refugio Peru and continues east through a series of rock fields until reaching the shore of a small lake. Keep your eyes and ears peeled for cairns marking the general path. After passing the small lake, the path starts an uphill climb with a series of tough switchbacks. There is a bit of a false summit after the switchbacks that would make for an excellent snack spot (-9.02523, -77.61725). Continue another half mile to the highest point on the trail before finishing the descent down to Laguna 69. As you descend, the lake will suddenly appear out of nowhere, revealing its deep blue color. Some of the best views of the lake are higher than the water level, so do not rush down to the water's edge before enjoying a rest at the higher viewpoints (-9.01479, -77.61111). Unfortunately, cloud cover hindered the dazzle given by the lake. But even with poor conditions, it was a gorgeous spot.

Laguna 69: 15,105 feet

From Laguna 69, it will take between two and three hours to hike down. You will enjoy the satisfaction of having completed a much wilder adventure than the majority of the hikers trying to reach the lake. Even though there are collectivos that travel past Cebellopampa on their way down to Yungay from Vaqueria, the easiest way to get a ride back to Yungay is with one of the day tour companies. Therefore, on your way down from Laguna 69, ask the guides hiking up if they have room to take you back into town. I had several guides offering me rides for only ten soles. This was much easier than the collectivo option. These guides will be more than happy to earn a little more money for no extra work on their part.

Volcán Chachani

Surrounding Peru's southern town of Arequipa are three towering volcanos, including El Misti, Pichu Pichu, and the tallest of them all, Chachani. Chachani and El Misti are the two most popular volcanos to climb around Arequipa, rising to 19,986 feet and 19,101 feet respectively. Chachani is even taller than Africa's highest mountain Kilimanjaro at 19,341 feet. The chance to ascend to over 6,000 meters above sea level is a fantastic opportunity for hikers ready to push the limit. The elevation of Chachani is the most important variable impacting the experience. Even though I had weeks of experience hiking at almost 17,000 feet, I knew that every additional thousand feet of altitude exponentially affects my body and threat of altitude sickness. The extreme elevation of Chachani was the principal force causing me to choose to hike with a guide and not attempt this independently. Altitude sickness is a serious threat to climbers who try to bite off more than they can chew as they attempt to reach the summit. I do not recommend completing either ascent without a guide because of the safety risk at such high altitudes. There also would be no way to reach the trailhead for the Chachani hike without having a vehicle. For me, having a guide for this high-altitude experience was a wise and rational choice.

With high altitude comes frigid temperatures. I typically am a hot-blooded hiker who prefers to wear as few layers as possible. This preference did not apply to Chachani. I was wearing every layer I had and still had cold toes. Full-size winter gloves are required, and a heavy winter coat would be a useful piece of gear.

Hiking Chachani doesn't provide the jaw dropping natural scenery compared to the Peruvian Andes. The allure of hiking Chachani is the thrill of reaching such high elevations and Mars-like terrain that feels like walking on another planet. Companies offer guided trips throughout Arequipa to both summits of El Misti and Chachani. My preference was to summit Chachani for the higher elevation and research indicating that El Misti is more severe in the slope's gradient, making it a tougher climb. For about $200, this was the most expensive two days of my entire trip. Even though I recommend joining a tour group for this hike, I will detail the itinerary to give you a comprehensive overview.

Volcán Chachani Trail Map

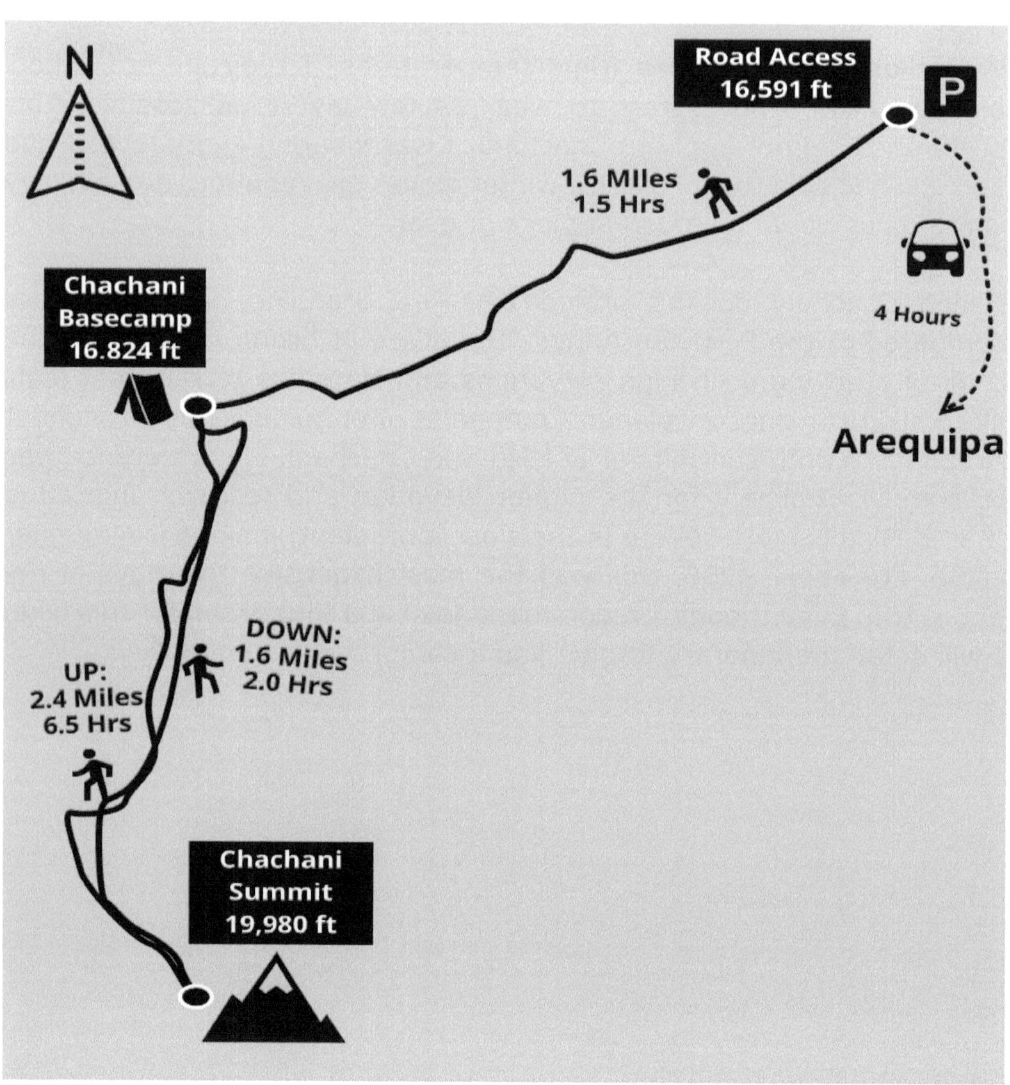

Recommended Itinerary: Chachani Summit

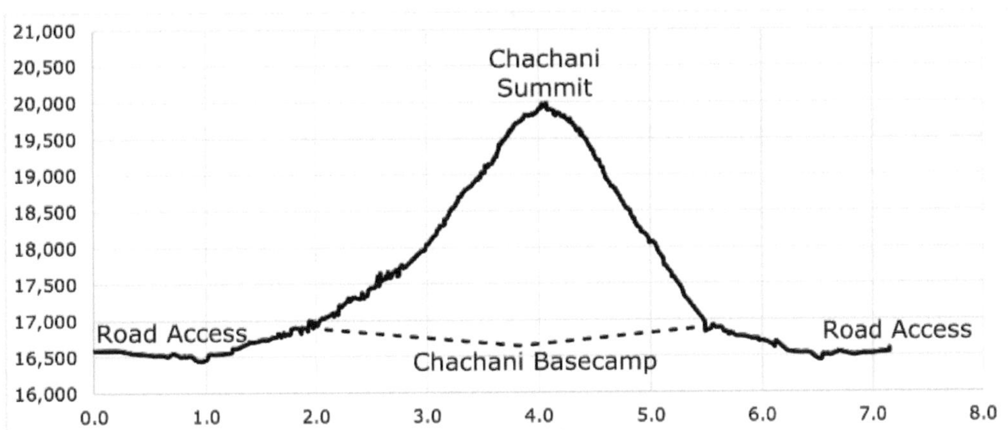

Day 1: Arequipa to Chachani Basecamp

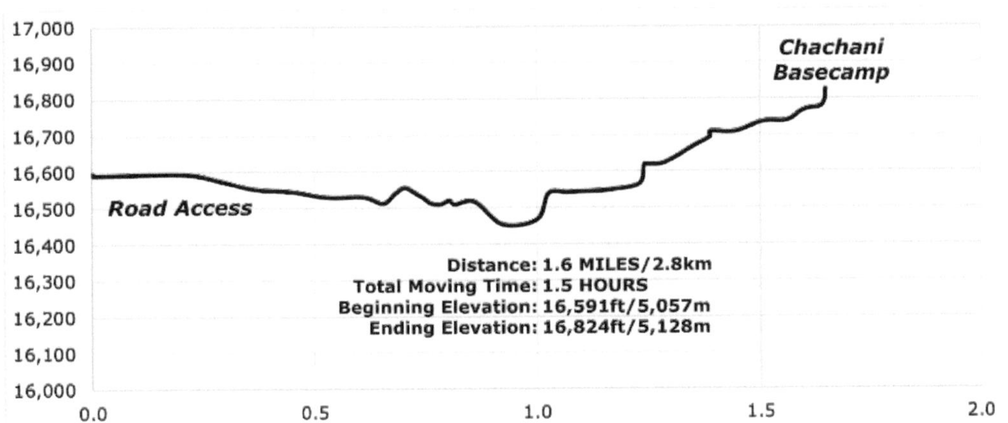

The first day of Chachani includes driving to the trailhead and hiking 1.6 miles with minimal elevation gain to the basecamp. It takes three to four hours of driving along bumpy dirt roads to get to the trailhead from Arequipa. The trailhead starts at almost 16,600 feet, almost as high as the tallest passes in both the Alpamayo Circuit and the Huayhuash Circuit. It is an easy 1.5 hour hike traversing over volcanic rock to the basecamp. The tour company owns the basecamp, so if you are attempting this independently, find another spot nearby. Enjoy an early dinner and sleep before the alarms go off very early to begin the summit climb.

Day 2: Chachani Summit. Return to Arequipa.

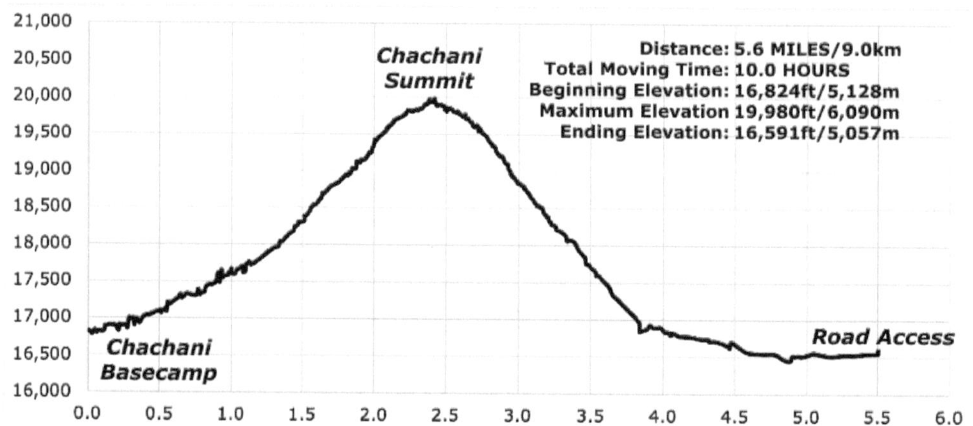

At 01:00, the alarms went off, and after a brief breakfast and hot tea, we began the ascent up to Chachani. The early wakeup is critical so that you reach the summit before midday and have ample time to get back down to basecamp before dark. The only things you need to take up to the summit are your warmest clothes, water, snacks, trekking poles, camera, and a headlamp. Hiking up in the pitch black with just a headlamp to illuminate the way is both an exhilarating and freezing cold experience. Our guide led the way up never-ending switchbacks on grainy volcanic rock until reaching the summit seven hours later. We spent the first four hours hiking in the freezing darkness and the remainder soaking in every beam of light emitted by the slowly rising sun. The Chachani summit is narrowly under 20,000 feet and offers gorgeous views of El Misti and Arequipa. It's a long day but well worth the experience.

Volcán Chachani Summit: 19,980 feet

Quick City Guides

These city guides will provide a brief introduction to the cities and provide recommendations on dining, lodging, and things to do. Maps are not included here. Check out my website, ***www.afineadventure.com***, to find Google Maps with all the waypoints marked. Please consult with additional resources on this topic as there are great crowdsourcing resources available.

Cusco

Cusco is Peru's second largest city with a population of 430,000. The city was the historic capital of the ancient Inca Empire from the 13th century until the 16th-century Spanish conquest. Cusco is the gateway for all adventures to the Salkantay Trek/Machu Picchu and Ausangate Trek. This red city is lined with red clay bricks that form the roads and buildings. Cusco is not an urban city like Lima. Minimal commercialization preserves the historic charm and provides tourists with the chance to experience life at 11,000 feet. Restaurants are abundant, shopping ranges from bargain markets to luxurious boutiques, and historical sites are well within walking distance.

Dining

Chakruna Native Burgers ($4-$8, -13.51478, -71.97437): Do not expect a McDonald's style burger at Chakruna Native Burger. I am a burger connessour so is not surprisingly that this was my favorite place to eat in Peru. *Chakruna Native Burgers* serves delicious Peruvian style burgers from a creative and modern kitchen. Vegetarians will love the variety of meat alternative options, including quinoa. Even though burgers are innately a Western staple, eating at Chakruna still felt like a unique and authentic Peruvian dining experience.

JC's Café ($7pp, -13.51574, -71.98359): Small café with inexpensive yet delicious food, both local Peruvian and Western options. A tranquil environment also provides some of the best coffee in town.

La Esquina ($6pp -13.51672, -71.9746): La Esquina serves fancy dessert options, including full ice cream sundaes. Comfortable sitting areas as well as delicious food and desserts make this a great spot to add to your Cusco dining plan.

Lodging

Ecopackers Hostel ($7pp, -13.51633, -71.98106): Located minutes from the Plaza des Aramas, Ecopackers Hostel served us well throughout our time in Cusco. It has everything you need, including quality WIFI, comfortable dorm rooms, and friendly English speaking staff that will help with everything you need. We enjoyed many delicious meals inside their bar at prices lower than most restaurants in the city. They also offered to store anything that we didn't need while we were out on the trek.

Points of Interest

Plaza des Armas (-13.51674, -71.97882): The city center of Cusco is the Plaza des Armas. This beautiful square block is surrounded by the Iglesia de la Compañia de Jesus and the Basílica Cathedral. On weekend mornings there are frequently large parades with local students playing in bands and other celebrations.

San Pedro Market (-13.52118, -71.98249): My favorite spot in Cusco is the vibrant San Pedro Market. This giant roofed market is a few blocks away from the Plaza des Armas and offers a variety of souvenir and produce vendors. Hikers planning on their next trek can create their own trail mix at one of the stands selling an array of nuts and dried fruits. Each day I was in Cusco I visited the San Pedro Market's outstanding juice bar. For a few soles, you can get a fresh mix of local fruits blended to make a heavenly drink. Prepare to haggle on souvenirs!

Christo Blanco Mirador (-13.50963, -71.97800): Perched high above Cusco is the iconic Christo Blanco, a towering statue and a great view of the Inca Valley. Christo Blanco Mirador is accessible by either hiking up or taxi.

Temple de la Luna (-13.50514, -71.96465): One of the free temples worth visiting in Cusco after the Christo Blanco is the Temple de la Luna. It is a fascinating ruin with historic stone structures.

Shopping

Souvenirs: There are countless places to buy souvenirs around the Plaza de Armas. As you wander around the side streets surrounding the Plaza, narrow alleys will lead to expansive courtyards lined with vendors selling all types of souvenirs including sweaters, blankets, t-shirts, and more. The San Pedro Market is the largest of all the souvenir markets.

If you enjoy artwork, there is a fantastic gallery at (-13.516144, -71.976673), where I almost pulled the trigger on a beautiful painting of Machu Picchu. Keep in mind that just about everything you find in the souvenir markets of Cusco can be found in any other city. So, if you want to reduce the amount of stuff you're lugging around, you might want to save your souvenir shopping until the end of your trip. Regardless, I recommend not buying anything until having a day to walk through all the markets and get a sense of all of the different options.

Outdoor Gear: For hiking gear, many small outfitters sell most everything you may have forgotten at home and need on the trail. My recommendation for equipment and apparel is a small outlet that sold us the bencina blanca required to fuel our MSR Dragonfly stove (-13.515225, -71.979733).

Grocery Store: Orion Supermarket (-13.51641, -71.98324)

Additional City Information

- City buses frequently run throughout the city, but taxis are a much easier form of transportation and are not expensive.
- Laundry services are plentiful and affordable anywhere near a hostel.
- Need cash? I recommend the BCP located on the Avenida El Sol (-13.518327, -71.978178).
- Broken Camera? There are camera repair shops near the corner of Avenida El Sol and Portal de Carnes that were able to fix my broken lens overnight.
- If you want to ship anything back home, the DHL on Avenida El Sol is the most reliable option (-13.52174,-71.975686). Be prepared for extremely high shipping rates.

Huaraz

Nestled in a valley surrounded by the Cordillera Blanca and Negro is the trekking capital of Peru, Huaraz. This city is the launching pad for hikes throughout the Cordillera Blanca and Huayhuash. Filled to the brim with hostels and restaurants, it is the perfect place to both prepare for the next hike as well as recover from the last. Rock climbing and mountaineering are additional options for visitors looking to cash-in a peak summit during their adventure. Huaraz was my favorite town throughout Peru because of the culture centered on backpacking. There are scores of companies offering day hiking and full circuit tours throughout the region.

Getting There

To get to Huaraz, take the eight-hour bus from Lima. All of the major bus companies make this route several times a day. You shouldn't need advanced reservations, but if you're on a tight schedule, it would be wise to purchase ahead of time. Take the overnight bus to save daylight for the fun part of traveling. For any taxi needs, like a ride to the Huayhuash or pickup from the bus station, contact my friend Freddy on WhatsApp (+51 932 181 032). He's so nice and helpful.

Dining

La Brasa Roja ($8pp, -9.53179, -77.52942): A large restaurant located a block south of Plaza de Armas is a great place to celebrate the completion of a major trek. An extensive range of menu options includes pizzas, burgers, and chicken. Significant portions make this a high value option frequented by both locals and tourists.

Antuco's Pizza ($10pp, -9.52837, -77.52861): A fire oven cooks delicious pizzas that pair well with a glass of wine or a pitcher of fresh squeezed lemonade. It will be hard to choose an entrée with so many possibilities. The warm, friendly atmosphere made this a favorite of Huaraz.

Café Andino ($5-$12pp, -9.5276, -77.52828): One of the most satisfying milkshakes is made at this high-level café. Come to this spot to research your next travel spot and enjoy a high-quality array of baked goods, western breakfast options, and hot drinks. The café is also a good place to buy trekking maps for the Cordillera Blanca and Huayhuash (80 soles for high quality topographic map).

Lodging

Aldo's Guest House ($8pp, -9.52825, -77.52814): Centrally located, affordably priced, and a beautiful rooftop view made this my basecamp for all travels around Huaraz. Besides that, the biggest value comes from the owner, Aldo himself. Aldo is a generous, friendly, English speaking gentleman who was extremely helpful talking about logistics for the different hikes. Relatively good WiFi and free breakfast are additional perks.

Points of Interest

Collectivo Station to Caraz (-9.52418, -77.52638): To get on a collectivo to Caraz or Yungay for the Alpamayo, Santa Cruz, Laguna Parón, and Laguna 69 hikes, you need to find this collectivo station. *The point marked on Maps.me is not correct!* The actual station is on 13 De Diciembre street just east of Jr. Cajamarca.

Monterrey Hot Springs ($3pp, -9.46881, -77.53617): This awesome oasis located about ten minutes outside of Huaraz is Peru's version of a waterpark. The large hot spring pools are a popular getaway for the locals. You can take a taxi for about 15 soles, or grab the #1 collectivo to Monterrey along Avenue Raymondi for about 2 soles (-9.52631, -77.52727).

Huascarán National Park Office (-9.53288, -77.53011): Before starting any hike throughout the Huascarán National Park, get your permit at this office. You can purchase permits at the various entrances to the park, but it is a good idea to be safe and buy them ahead of time just in case.

Bank/ATM (-9.52933, -77.52902): The best place to withdraw cash is the BCP on Avenida Mariscal Toribio de Luzuriaga near the northwest corner of the Plaza de Armas.

Shopping

Novaplaza Grocery Store (-9.52830, -77.52758): There are many grocery stores in Huaraz, but this was the best for its supply of backpacking food. They had a great supply of packaged meats perfect for the trail.

Feria Artesanal La Plaza (-9.52996, -77.52843): Looking for souvenirs? On the east side of the Plaza de Armas is the only souvenir market in Huaraz. You will find a lot of the same things in Lima or Cusco, just with Huaraz printed instead.

Ferretería (-9.52616, -77.52921): If you need bencina blanca for a camping stove, don't waste money buying it from an outfitter. Along Avenue Raymondi west of Avenida Mariscal Toribio de Luzuriaga are a series of different Ferreterías (hardware stores) that should be able to sell you a liter bottle for about $2.50.

Caraz

Caraz is the launching point for the Alpamayo Circuit, Santa Cruz Trek, and Laguna Parón hike. Smaller than Huaraz, you will not find anywhere near as good of dining, lodging, and shopping opportunities. However, I still recommend staying overnight in Caraz before starting any of these hikes to save you from an unbearably long and early day starting in Huaraz. Far fewer tourists are found in Caraz compared to Huaraz.

Getting There

Caraz can be reached from Huaraz by collectivo. The collectivo leaves Huaraz about every fifteen to twenty minutes. These packed mini vans are a worthwhile cultural experience and costs 7 soles.

Dining

Dining options are severely limited in Caraz. Around the main markets are some delicious street food options that I enjoyed the most from all the dining experiences in Caraz. Fried chicken, beef kabobs, and more can be found for those willing to dare eating street food.

Lodging

Casa Salazar ($9 per room, -9.04530, -77.80696): My stay at Casa Salazar was quite enjoyable. It is not a social hostel. Instead, there are only private rooms available with shared bathrooms. Pros: Opportunity to have a private room after endless dorm experiences, the willingness of owner to store items not needed during treks, and an excellent location near the major markets. Cons: Poor hot water.

Shopping

Mercado Central (-9.04679, -77.80921): The main supermarkets have tons of produce and other goods. It is where all the locals do their shopping for everything from sneakers to bananas. I had no problem buying fresh avocados and oranges but did have trouble finding food I could cook and pack out on the trail. The best trail food I could find were small packages of pasta and tomato sauce that came in a small pouch. Ask around, and there are even a few vendors who sell packets of parmesan cheese. Try to do as much food shopping for the treks in Huaraz before arriving in Caraz. You'll find cookies and other junk food, but few optimal hiking snacks and "real" food options.

Points of Interest

Collectivo to Cashapampa and Parón (-9.04640, -77.80724)

Collectivo to Yungay and Huaraz (-9.05119, -77.80933)

Bank: BCP (-9.04823, -77.81086)

Paracas

One of the astonishing features of Peru is its diversity of landscapes. Paracas is a small oceanside town 125 miles south of Lima that will genuinely make you question whether you are in the same country as the one you've hiked up 17,000 feet. After weeks of backpacking in high alpine conditions, Paracas offers the chance for visitors to escape down to sea level and have a completely different experience. The southern stretch of Peru is marked by extremely arid land and desert. Sand peaks replace ice capped mountains, and glacial lakes are replaced by the Pacific Ocean. Paracas can be reached by bus from either the north or south direction. A three hour bus route connects Lima and Paracas from the north and Paracas can be reached via Ica from the south.

Paracas's proximity to the ocean steers the entire local economy and cuisine. Peruvian ceviche, a seafood medley dish, can be found throughout Peru, but the absolute best is located right next to the source. When you're in an oceanside town, seafood is going to be the most authentic cuisine available. The expensive tourist restaurants are easy to spot along the main plaza pier. Enjoy a drink or two at any of these places where "happy hour" seems to last all day long. But for food, there are tons of smaller cheaper food stands just a block further south where the ceviche is just as good.

Everything in Paracas is a bit more expensive than the rest of Peru. Tour guides will spot you on their radar as soon as you get off the bus and try desperately to get your business. Before paying any tour company, ensure that they are licensed to operate, and that all of the included portions of the tour are in writing. I highly recommend James from Pisco Tours. Check out their site at www.piscotravel.com.

Points of Interest

Islas Ballestas ($12pp): The largest tourist attraction in Paracas is the Islas Ballestas. These small islands off the coast of Paracas are home to countless marine wildlife, including sea lions, Humboldt penguins, and Peruvian boobies. Boat tours take tourists along the shores to marvel at the millions of birds that inhabit the islands as well as the adorable sea lions lounging on the rocks. The tour is worth the price. Tours typically cost 25 soles, but there is an additional national park entrance fee of 22 soles. Book a tour with one of the reputable agencies in town. On the way to the islands, the boats stop at the Paracas Candelabra. This pre-historic geoglyph of a chandelier carved in the desert ground still leaves researchers guessing as to why it was created.

Paracas National Reserve: South of Paracas is home to the Paracas National Reserve, an enormous span of oceanside deserts and beaches. There are many ways to visit the National Reserve. Tour buses offer rides to each of the main attractions, or the most adventurous can take bikes or even dune buggies! Since this guide's focus is on trekking, full details on how to plan your day trip through the Paracas National Reserve can be found on my website, ***www.afineadventure.com***.

Huacachina

Nestled inside the expansive deserts around Ica is a hidden oasis called Huacachina, a small town filled to the brim with hostels and restaurants surrounding a tiny lake in the middle of the desert. The main attraction of Huacachina, and frankly, the only reason to tolerate innumerable tourists is the tremendously fun sand dune buggy rides. Great fun! For about $40, you get to take a two-hour ride on a giant dune buggy as the driver rides up and down the slopes of the desert sand like an amusement park.

There are no public buses directly to Huacachina. To get there, take a bus to nearby Ica and then hire a taxi for the 15 minute ride.

Nazca

The next stop south from Huacachina is Nazca. A stop in Nazca is only necessary if you have an interest in seeing the Nazca Lines. The Nazca Lines are a group of gigantic geoglyphs formed by shallow depressions in the soil of the Nazca desert. The lines create almost perfect depictions of animals like a hummingbird and a monkey, as well as geometric shapes. The geoglyphs are so large that it is impossible to view them from the ground. Only seen from a plane do the Nazca Lines come to life and reveal their extraordinary size and accuracy. Seeing the Nazca Lines is one of the more expensive ticket items on my Peru trip, running close to $100 for the thirty-minute plane ride. Despite the hefty price tag, I highly recommend the experience to see this wonder for yourself. Visit the Nazca Planetarium for a fascinating tour explaining the relationship between the lines and astronomy.

<u>***Arequipa***</u>

Also known as "The White City," Arequipa is a beautiful place surrounded by three volcanos, including Chachani and El Misti. The second most populated city in Peru behind Lima, Arequipa offers visitors the chance to see some beautiful Spanish architecture and has great adventure activities within close proximity. Arequipa feels similar to Cusco, but red clay is replaced with white stone. Visit Arequipa for a great city experience with a lot of history and fun things to do.

See the chapter on climbing Volcán Chachani for more details. Another popular activity from Arequipa is a visit to the Colca Canyon. Time restrictions unfortunately forced me to choose between the two highlights. If time permits for you, definitely plan on 2-4 days of hiking through Peru's version of the Grand Canyon.

Lima

Peru's capital of Lima, for me, was unfortunately limited to just last minute souvenir shopping at the Inka Plaza as well as the airport where I concluded my adventure and headed home. Some side effects from the harsh adjustment of descending 20,000 feet over just 24 hours severely limited my ability to explore this city. Please see additional resources specifically for Lima, but I hope to provide a few details that will be useful.

Lima is separated into districts, each with its own style and characteristics. The two most popular areas of Lima for visitors are Miraflores and Barranco. Both areas are far south of the airport. A taxi from the airport to Miraflores cost about 50 soles, or you can take a bus with Airport Express Lima for half the cost at just 25 soles. To buy a bus ticket, you'll find a stand for the bus company near baggage claim. There are two major bus terminals, Plaza Norte in the northern part of Lima and Javier Prado to the south. Depending on where you are traveling to and from, the buses typically drop off at either stop.

The best souvenir shopping throughout all of Peru is found at Inka Plaza in Miraflores. You can easily spend an entire day looking through each stall to find the perfect gift for all your friends and family. This is where I did all of my souvenir shopping for the whole trip. Souvenirs are pretty generic throughout Peru. You will quickly recognize the same blankets, jackets, and more at different stalls around the country. I would only buy souvenirs if it is something truly unique to the city you are in, or if it is your last destination before heading home.

There is a great art section of the market where you'll find fantastic local artists showcasing their work. But I found that none of the artwork related to my experience hiking throughout the Andes. An artist recognized the lack of paintings available with mountains and offered to paint any scene I wanted. Overnight, the artist painted the spectacular landscape from the Mirador de las Tres Lagunas on the Huayhuash Circuit for me off of a picture I provided. Absolutely incredible!

Two Month Peru Trip Cost

Category	Cost
Camping/Lodging	$ 337
Food	$ 536
Transportation	$ 348
Flight	$ 147
Gear	$ 230
Souvenirs	$ 309
Activities	$ 460
Misc	$ 101
TOTAL	**$2,467**

For about $40 per day I was able to have the adventure of a lifetime. A few important notes about the costs. First, notice that my flights were only $147. This is because most of my flight cost was paid for with airline miles. The second worth mentioning is that about $200 of the gear cost was to fix my camera lens that broke midway through the trip. Another $200 was solely dedicated to the only guided trip I did to the summit of Volcán Chachani. The point here is to give you a sense of how affordable traveling to Peru truly is, and the economic benefit of choosing to travel independently. Your costs will be highly dictated by your spending choices along the way and the trip's duration. I consider keeping overall daily travel costs less than $50 per day a huge success. For some more perspective on the benefits of hiking independently, Backpacker Magazine currently offers a guided eight days/seven nights trip to the Huayhuash Circuit for $3,500 per person! The egregious cost of guided treks from nonlocal companies is staggering. Even if you prefer the guided trek option, find a local company that will offer much more competitive rates. The highest cost of the trip for me is almost always food. Food in Peru is affordable, ranging from dinners for a couple dollars to the most lavish meal experienced for $25.

International Travel

Flying Internationally

Congratulations! You are embarking on an international journey to Peru. Flying internationally is much more involved than domestic, with more obstacles and considerations. Here are a few lessons integral to successfully making it to your final destination.

- Checked baggage needs to be picked up and processed through customs as soon as you enter your destination country, not necessarily your destination city. For example, if your flight to Cusco from the US goes through Lima, you will have to take your checked luggage through customs in Lima and then recheck the bag for the final flight to Cusco. You'll be disappointed if you assumed your bags would be waiting for you in Cusco and learn they are sitting in Lima. Certain countries have a designated recheck-in location for this, but in others, you have to go through the whole check-in process again for the final leg.
- Do not strap items such as tents and hiking poles to the outside of your pack and expect them to be there when you pick them up. Even if they are securely attached, it will not stop a thief. Many airlines will wrap your pack in plastic to protect the straps and keep the bag clean upon request. Ask for an extra bag to carry with you for the trip back home.
- Customs will stamp your passport and give you some form of a receipt. Make sure to keep the receipt with you for the duration of your trip. Many countries will want the receipt upon your departure from the country, and lodging often requires it upon check-in.
- Do not trust that an airline generated flight itinerary will provide you with sufficient layover time. At least a 90-minute layover is recommended for all international segments, particularly when you are entering your destination country since you need extra

time to get through customs. Travel sites will generate an itinerary that theoretically will work but might force you to sprint through the airport to make the next leg. And that's if everything goes right beforehand.

- Make sure that your passport is not only valid upon your departure and return, but for an extended period after your scheduled return. Different countries have different regulations on how long your passport must be valid beyond the dates of your trip, usually around three months.

Cash or Credit? How to Handle $$ Internationally

Traveling in another country with foreign currency is a game with many moving parts. Think of foreign currency as another good that you are buying for the trip. When you use an ATM, you are paying the local bank a certain amount of your local currency for the foreign currency. The "price" of this foreign currency is based on current exchange rates as well as transaction fees assigned by both the foreign bank to give you foreign currency and your home bank to convert its currency to the foreign bank. Just like picking a hotel, if you are getting the same product, in this case, a fixed amount of foreign currency, you want to buy it at the lowest price.

In most foreign countries, a majority of financial transactions are made in cash, while other countries have a greater ability to process credit cards. Knowing the policies and fees on your credit cards and ATMs will dictate the best way for you to spend money. Travel credit cards with your preferred airline are a great way to accumulate rewards for travel and to save on foreign transaction fees. In general, if you can use a travel credit card with no fee, do it. The credit card likely has a better conversion rate compared to what you will get from a foreign bank's ATM.

However, not every merchant will accept credit cards and will require local currency. ATM withdrawals can quickly become a considerable expense with no reward. Typically, the foreign bank and your home bank will both charge you a flat fee for every withdrawal. Research options with local credit unions that offer a small percentage fee for each withdrawal instead of a flat rate. That way, there is no inhibitor to making multiple withdrawals throughout the trip.

When withdrawing from an ATM, there is a balance between taking too much and too little cash out. Take out too little cash, and you will have to withdraw again and possibly incur another fee. Take out too much, and you are at higher risk of having your money lost or stolen. The goal is for you not to be left with any foreign currency upon departure. Currency exchange companies are notoriously cheap and will offer far less for the same money as you paid for it. If you are left with cash, avoid currency exchanges at the airport and try to exchange cash at local banks in the city. For any credit or debit card you plan on using internationally, make sure to alert your bank in advance to prevent the unwanted closure of your account.

In Peru, credit cards are widely accepted at restaurants, lodging, and gas stations. Try to use your credit card as much as possible. If it does not have foreign transaction fees, you will get the best conversion rate. Sometimes merchants require a minimum charge to use a credit card. Cash will still be needed for other purchases.

International Phone Service

Depending on your phone carrier, there will be different options for international phone service. Most plans now have two options: a cheaper alternative that is a flat monthly fee with unlimited texting and a small data package or a higher daily fee to keep your same plan as you have at home. I recommend the cheaper option and choose WiFi for all data needs. After all, you're here to experience nature, not

Facebook! Make sure that data consuming applications are switched off of data in your phone settings as well as iMessage for iPhone users.

Traveler's Insurance

Traveler's insurance provides protection for different risks associated with the trip, mainly personal health and financial. Plans and coverages vary significantly by the provider. The first reason to get traveler's insurance is that most health insurance policies do not cover international travel. If you get hurt in a remote area and have to go to the hospital, you could be responsible for some major medical bills. Make sure to get a plan that has substantial medical coverage. The second reason to purchase traveler's insurance is to protect you financially. Certain unforeseen events can occur, preventing you from going on the trip, such as a family member's death or personal injury where you will be paid back for the monetary value of the trip. Many insurance plans protect you financially by reimbursing you for missed flight connections and lost/stolen belongings. Most plans can be upgraded to include rental car coverage.

Just like all insurance, the greater the protection, the greater the premium. Factors such as the duration of the trip, estimated monetary value of the trip, and how far in advance the trip is made prior to being insured will change the price of insurance. InsureMyTrip.com is a great resource to compare costs and coverages across different providers. They offer a variety of resources to help you decide which coverage is best for you and understand the terms. Check with your credit card company as well to see what coverage they provide for international travel.

Packing a Backpack

There is a lot of gear you need to stuff into your pack. The position and placement of your gear will make a difference in your comfort and balance while hiking. Follow these guidelines to pack efficiently:

- Cushiony stuff on the bottom! The lower compartment of your pack will be in direct contact with your back and is for soft things like the sleeping bag and pad. Bury items you only need at night.
- Above this soft layer should be heavier items like cookware and food. Keeping the center of gravity low on your pack will help its balance. But have that day's snack and lunch readily available for quick access upon stopping.
- Stay organized! Pack clothes into stuff sacks and group items into categories. You should know where every item is inside your pack. Find a system that works for you and replicate that every morning when you pack up camp.
- Keep rain gear and a warm layer in a quick access compartment or at the top of your pack ready to go. Rain and cold winds can come without notice, be prepared!
- Make sure all food is packed in a sealed container that doesn't risk rupture. Reinforce caps with duct tape so you don't get precious hot sauce all over your sleeping bag!
- Before you start hiking, put the pack on and make sure it feels secure and well balanced. Over the course of a day, an unbalanced pack slowly causes unnecessary strain on your body.

Conclusion

Peru is an extraordinary country where the trekking opportunities are limitless. My objective is that this guide has provided you a comprehensive understanding of how to independently complete many of the major treks Peru has to offer. It is always going to be impossible to create an all-inclusive guide to anywhere in the world. Travel bloggers love using "ultimate guide" when describing their content. The truth is that none of us has the ultimate knowledge of anywhere. Continue researching, reach out to multiple resources, and gain more perspectives from the rest of the travel community. This guide should be one of many resources you use in planning a trip to Peru.

Turn your bucket list into a doing list. With all of life's responsibilities, deadlines, commitments, there will always be a million reasons to say no. Saying yes to adventure takes courage. I believe that it is through these experiences that people truly develop into the best version of themselves. Whether you can spend a week or three months away, Peru will give you treasured memories to last a lifetime.

I love connecting with my readers. Head to **www.afineadventure.com** and connect with me on all the social media. Please feel free to reach out to me with any questions; I'd be happy to consult with you about your trip. If you found this book helpful, please give it a 5 star review so that other prospective travelers might benefit from it as well. Thank you for reading and have an unforgettable adventure!

Questions or Comments? Send me a note at
andyfineadventure@gmail.com

Appendix

GPS Waypoints and Elevations

Alpamayo Circuit					
Waypoint	**Location**	**Latitude**	**Longitude**	**Elevation (ft)**	**Elevation (m)**
1	Cashapampa	-8.956958	-77.777345	9,619	2,932
2	Cashapampa Ranger Station	-8.953988	-77.775452	9,692	2,954
3	Water Access	-8.956147	-77.748629	11,368	3,465
4	Llamacoral Campground	-8.946018	-77.700697	12,172	3,710
5	Jatunquisuar Campground	-8.915545	-77.623153	13,077	3,986
6	Alpamayo South Basecamp	-8.892878	-77.633839	14,229	4,337
7	Laguna Arhuaycocha	-8.889500	-77.631862	14,521	4,426
8	Taullipampa Campground	-8.918305	-77.607920	13,593	4,143
9	Punta Union Pass	-8.912566	-77.581897	15,690	4,782
10	Fork (Santa Cruz vs. Alpamayo Circuit)	-8.921221	-77.563909	14,170	4,319
11	Tuctupampa Campground	-8.923580	-77.558713	13,668	4,166
12	Alto de Pucaraju	-8.917839	-77.553650	15,190	4,630
13	Laguna Huercrococha Area Campground	-8.919287	-77.511680	12,635	3,851
14	Lake Near Tupatupa Pass	-8.888076	-77.522669	13,845	4,220
15	Tupatupa Pass	-8.884309	-77.520786	14,313	4,363
16	Jancapampa Small Shop	-8.850422	-77.522033	11,545	3,519
17	Jancapampa Campground	-8.851717	-77.550512	11,631	3,545
18	River Crossing	-8.839127	-77.555929	12,451	3,795
19	Yanacon Pass	-8.826637	-77.589800	15,125	4,610
20	Huillca Campground	-8.806667	-77.608826	13,133	4,003
21	Fork	-8.811587	-77.624966	13,445	4,098
22	Mesapata Pass	-8.810583	-77.635686	14,650	4,465

23	Gara Gara Pass	-8.825984	-77.673665	15,922	4,853
24	Jancarurish Campground	-8.846233	-77.681603	13,878	4,230
25	Alpamayo Base Camp North	-8.863460	-77.679829	14,754	4,497
26	River Crossing	-8.867464	-77.682384	14,902	4,542
27	Beginning of Steep Ascent	-8.878486	-77.690630	15,525	4,732
28	Santa Cruz Sanctuary	-8.880939	-77.697771	16,473	5,021
29	River crossing	-8.837059	-77.702310	13,625	4,153
30	Ruinapampa Campground	-8.828700	-77.733236	13,163	4,012
31	Vientunan Pass	-8.843250	-77.746391	15,617	4,760
32	Osuri II Campground	-8.845652	-77.749298	15,253	4,649
33	Osuri Main Campground	-8.846041	-77.752333	14,895	4,540
34	Osuri Pass	-8.857681	-77.755260	15,948	4,861
35	Osuri Viewpoint	-8.858381	-77.753416	16,148	4,922
36	Yuraaccocha Trail Fork	-8.866727	-77.773971	14,524	4,427
37	Yuraccocha Trail Pass	-8.880544	-77.773080	15,194	4,631
38	Laguna Yuraccocha Campground	-8.884319	-77.735985	15,233	4,643
39	Huishcash Campground	-8.867029	-77.778066	14,121	4,304
40	Camp Calaminas	-8.876549	-77.785252	13,068	3,983
41	Hualcayán	-8.897456	-77.799768	10,324	3,147

Ausangate Trek					
Waypoint	Location	Latitude	Longitude	Elevation (feet)	Elevation (meters)
1	Tinki	-13.666859	-71.321712	12,471	3,801
2	Abra Khampa	-13.767983	-71.176581	16,640	5,072
3	Arapa Pass	-13.776155	-71.274617	15,604	4,756
4	Laguna Pucacocha Viewpoint	-13.806802	-71.280832	15,066	4,592
5	Jatun Pucacocha Campground	-13.815617	-71.267800	15,501	4,725
6	Ausangate Pass	-13.825447	-71.266655	16,378	4,992
7	Anata Campground	-13.841517	-71.284133	15,686	4,781
8	Abra Warmisaya	-13.844966	-71.290545	16,444	5,012
9	Unclear Path to Rainbow Mtn	-13.851814	-71.293312	15,768	4,806
10	Montana Winkunka/Rainbow Mtn	-13.867868	-71.302982	16,503	5,030
11	Quesiuno Campground	-13.873400	-71.241733	14,209	4,331
12	Ausangatecocha Campground	-13.825282	-71.237945	15,167	4,623
13	Palomani Pass	-13.816771	-71.222730	16,766	5,110
14	Camp Pampacancha	-13.824351	-71.189851	14,665	4,470
15	Jampa Campground	-13.803722	-71.169494	15,040	4,584
16	Fork Stay Left	-13.762896	-71.198226	15,919	4,852
17	Lake Viewpoint	-13.763832	-71.212365	15,522	4,731
18	Water Jump	-13.758769	-71.225389	15,049	4,587
19	Pacchanta	-13.718772	-71.241614	14,226	4,336
20	Upis Campground	-13.751645	-71.274072	14,850	4,526

Huayhuash Circuit					
Waypoint	**Location**	**Latitude**	**Longitude**	**Elevation (feet)**	**Elevation (meters)**
1	Quartelhuain Trailhead	-10.155230	-76.923695	13,652	4,161
2	Cacanapunta Pass	-10.156505	-76.911676	15,390	4,691
3	Janca Campground	-10.180111	-76.890627	13,937	4,248
4	Mitococha Campground	-10.193918	-76.894785	14,050	4,282
5	Carhuac Pass	-10.211615	-76.873138	15,174	4,625
6	Carhuacocha Campground	-10.240781	-76.861275	13,707	4,178
7	Laguna Gangrajanca Viewpoint	-10.269662	-76.872541	14,272	4,350
8	Mirador de los tres Lagunas	-10.284897	-76.864526	14,951	4,557
9	Siula Pass	-10.287499	-76.855580	15,860	4,834
10	Huayhuash Campground	-10.327950	-76.843215	14,268	4,349

11	Challenging Terrain. Caution	-10.221893	-76.886624	15,768	4,806
12	Mitococha Viewpoint	-10.196289	-76.890072	15,000	4,572
13	Trepacio Pass Waypoint	-10.348400	-76.850817	15,089	4,599
14	Trepacio Pass	-10.347899	-76.874047	16,555	5,046
15	Glacier Viewpoint	-10.343861	-76.875870	16,845	5,134
16	Cuyoc Campground	-10.375569	-76.893531	14,795	4,510
17	Portachuelo Pass	-10.372250	-76.844667	15,695	4,784
18	Viconga Campground	-10.412612	-76.852031	14,529	4,428
19	Cuyoc Pass	-10.393767	-76.879317	16,516	5,034
20	Santa Rosa Pass	-10.354667	-76.894090	16,663	5,079
21	San Antonio Pass	-10.356514	-76.898733	16,462	5,018
22	Laguna Jurau Viewpoint	-10.337326	-76.892840	14,083	4,292
23	Cutatambo Campground	-10.343553	-76.901893	14,049	4,282
24	Siula Viewpoint	-10.314311	-76.915078	15,194	4,631
25	Rosario Viewpoint with Stacked Boulder	-10.318106	-76.922825	16,580	5,054
26	Rosario Pass	-10.316042	-76.924205	16,845	5,134
27	Laguna Caramarca Campground	-10.294961	-76.930003	15,077	4,595
28	Warning! Glacier and sketchy rock scramble	-10.278087	-76.932208	16,800	5,121
29	Rasac Pass	-10.277517	-76.932800	16,818	5,126
30	Rasac Viewpoint	-10.275700	-76.936217	16,594	5,058
31	Jauacocha Campground	-10.236146	-76.965215	13,444	4,098
32	Mini Mirador Cerro Huacrish	-10.242141	-76.973817	14,944	4,555
33	Llamac Pass	-10.224762	-77.012103	14,160	4,316
34	Pampa Llamac	-10.223184	-77.022688	13,996	4,266
35	Mirador Cerro Huacrish	-10.246144	-76.976583	15,798	4,815
36	Tapush Pass	-10.292233	-76.999117	15,646	4,769
37	LLaucha Pass	-10.268259	-76.976689	15,903	4,847
38	Huayllapa Campground	-10.357233	-76.996883	11,853	3,613

39	Huatiaq Campground	-10.325883	-76.994800	14,154	4,314
40	Gashapampa Campground	-10.273738	-76.996941	14,876	4,534
41	Wanacpatay Campground	-10.376345	-76.937320	14,198	4,328
42	Llamac to Huaraz Bus Station	-10.197883	-77.032583	10,712	3,265
43	Llamac	-10.198730	-77.033244	10,712	3,265

Laguna 69/Pisco Basecamp					
Waypoint	**Location**	**Latitude**	**Longitude**	**Elevation (feet)**	**Elevation (meters)**
1	Lake Llanganuco Campground	-9.051973	-77.618730	12,671	3,862
2	Cebellopampa Trailhead and Bus Parking Lot	-9.045825	-77.609266	12,817	3,907
3	Pisco Basecamp Campground	-9.030949	-77.630218	15,225	4,641
4	Refugio Perú	-9.029753	-77.629437	15,272	4,655
5	False Summit	-9.025233	-77.617254	15,883	4,841
6	Pisco Pass	-9.020867	-77.611283	15,994	4,875
7	Laguna 69 Viewpoint	-9.014793	-77.611118	15,594	4,753
8	Laguna 69	-9.011989	-77.610942	15,105	4,604

Laguna Parón					
Waypoint	**Location**	**Latitude**	**Longitude**	**Elevation (feet)**	**Elevation (meters)**
1	Laguna Parón Control Station	-9.038430	-77.732440	11,000	3,353
2	Turn Left Uphill	-8.985047	-77.657391	13,781	4,200
3	Laguna Parón Campground	-8.985310	-77.654734	13,781	4,200
4	Mirador Laguna Parón	-9.000543	-77.681982	14,196	4,327

Salkantay Trek					
Waypoint	Location	Latitude	Longitude	Elevation (feet)	Elevation (meters)
1	Mollepata	-13.508601	-72.528433	9,376	2,858
2	Mirador Chinchirkuma	-13.451200	-72.548920	12,448	3,794
3	Soryapampa Campground	-13.386848	-72.574120	12,959	3,950
4	Laguna Humantay	-13.381093	-72.584507	13,976	4,260
5	Salkantaypampa Campground	-13.369227	-72.562052	13,641	4,158
6	Abra Salkantay	-13.348583	-72.563314	15,279	4,657
7	Wayramachay Campground	-13.321813	-72.607655	12,323	3,756
8	Chaullay Campground	-13.324489	-72.664481	9,508	2,898
9	Collpapampa Campground	-13.317809	-72.669003	9,295	2,833
10	River Crossing	-13.316427	-72.667998	8,888	2,709
11	Winaypocca Campground	-13.296466	-72.649113	8,012	2,442
12	Llaqta Campground	-13.278960	-72.645919	7,917	2,413
13	Sawayaco Campground	-13.226585	-72.628040	6,759	2,060
14	Llactapata Control Point	-13.213617	-72.617383	6,575	2,004
15	Llactapata Lodge	-13.185654	-72.581489	8,478	2,584
16	Hidroelétrica	-13.174809	-72.559943	5,893	1,796
17	Hiking Entrance to Machu Picchu	-13.161808	-72.535933	6,734	2,053
18	Aguas Calientes	-13.154260	-72.527825	7,010	2,137
19	Machu Picchu Ruins Entrance	-13.165816	-72.543149	7,969	2,429
20	Montana Machu Picchu	-13.174661	-72.542074	10,040	3,060
21	Santa Teresa	-13.130222	-72.594048	5,138	1,566
22	Santa Teresa Thermal Springs	-13.109667	-72.600707	4,590	1,399
23	Machu Picchu Ticket Office	-13.154184	-72.525316	7,010	2,137

Volcán Chachani					
Waypoint	**Location**	**Latitude**	**Longitude**	**Elevation (feet)**	**Elevation (meters)**
1	Volcán Chachani Basecamp	-16.176155	-71.532755	16,819	5,126
2	Road Access Point	-16.167411	-71.512391	16,591	5,057
3	Chachani Summit	-16.195182	-71.531985	19,980	6,090

Caraz			
Category	**Location**	**Latitude**	**Longitude**
Transport	Collectivo - Caraz Huaraz	-9.051199	-77.809334
Transport	Collectivo to Cashapampa and Parón	-9.046406	-77.807244
Shopping	Ferretería - Bencina Blanca	-9.048348	-77.809612
Shopping	Mercado	-9.046798	-77.808404
Shopping	Mercado Central	-9.046796	-77.809215
Shopping	Mercado La Explanada	-9.046851	-77.807579
Lodging	Casa Salazar	-9.045301	-77.806960
Bank	BCP - Bank/ATM	-9.048232	-77.810868

Cusco			
Category	**Location**	**Latitude**	**Longitude**
Transport	Bus to Tinki AUSANGATE TREK	-13.527045	-71.958118
Food	Jack's Café	-13.515617	-71.975690
Food	Chakruna Native Burgers	-13.514787	-71.974375
Food	JC's Cafe	-13.515745	-71.983591
Food	Pankracio	-13.516201	-71.982075
Food	Los Toldos Chicken	-13.519218	-71.978802
Food	Crepería & Backpacker La Bo'M	-13.513735	-71.976221
Transport	Alejandro Velasco Astete Airport	-13.537636	-71.943614
Shopping	San Pedro Market - Produce & Souvenirs	-13.521187	-71.982496

Shopping	Orión Supermercados - Groceries	-13.516415	-71.983246
POI	Plaza De Armas	-13.516746	-71.978824
POI	Cathedral of Santo Domingo	-13.515442	-71.976553
POI	Mirador desde el Cristo Blanco	-13.509631	-71.978006
POI	Temple de la Luna	-13.505141	-71.964651
Lodging	Ecopackers	-13.516330	-71.981060
POI	U.S. Consular Office	-13.520244	-71.976789

Huaraz			
Category	**Location**	**Latitude**	**Longitude**
Transport	Bus to Yungay	-9.524186	-77.526389
Transport	Bus to Chiquian	-9.532076	-77.532148
Transport	Bus to Monterrey Hot Springs	-9.526312	-77.527277
Transport	Oltursa Bus Lima	-9.526078	-77.527387
POI	POST OFFICE	-9.529628	-77.529322
POI	Monterrey Hot Springs	-9.468811	-77.536172
Shopping	Feria Artesanal La Plaza - Souvenirs	-9.529962	-77.528432
Shopping	Novaplaza -Groceries	-9.528306	-77.527587
Shopping	Ferretería for Bencina Blanca	-9.526165	-77.529217
POI	Huascarán National Park Office	-9.532883	-77.530117
Bank	Banco de Crédito del Perú - ATM	-9.529338	-77.529022
Food	La Brasa Roja	-9.531793	-77.529428
Food	EL RINCONCITO MINERO	-9.528065	-77.527884
Food	Pizzeria Grill El Horno	-9.529042	-77.528145
Food	Café Andino	-9.527609	-77.528285
Food	Mi Comedia - Pizzeria	-9.521244	-77.529211
Food	Chilli Heaven	-9.528870	-77.528222
Food	Foode "LA CASITA RUSTIKA"	-9.532885	-77.520478
Food	Rossonero Gelato Café	-9.528671	-77.528993

Food	Antuco	-9.528380	-77.528618
Food	El Tambo	-9.527606	-77.527628
Food	Makondos Zona Vip	-9.527692	-77.527016
Food	El Tío Enrique	-9.528053	-77.527509
Lodging	Akilpo Hostel	-9.526171	-77.530166
Lodging	AndesCamp Hostel & Expeditions	-9.532800	-77.532511
Lodging	Aldo's Guest House	-9.528254	-77.528143

About the Author

Andy Fine has been traveling the world since his first international trip to France in 2004. Since, he has traveled to 19 countries across five continents. As of this second edition's publication, he has been to China, Thailand, Hong Kong, Vietnam, Japan, Australia, France, England, Greece, the British and US Virgin Islands, Costa Rica, Canada, United States, Chile, Argentina, Peru, Israel, Jordan, Switzerland, and Italy! His love for the outdoors and camping came from his 13 years of experience as a camper and ultimately a trips counselor at Camp Leelanau for Boys in Maple City, Michigan. As a certified Wilderness First Responder and trained Experiential Education leader, Andy has had great opportunities to learn what it takes to successfully trek throughout the world. During the day, Andy works in the Pricing and Revenue Management Department at United Airlines. Andy operates the blog, **www.afineadventure.com**, where he posts guides and tips for traveling to the places he has been so far. When he is not traveling or camping, Andy enjoys sailing, skiing, tennis, and biking.

Top Left Going Counterclockwise
Torres del Paine National Park, Chile
Emerald Lake, Yoho National Park, Canada
Yosemite National Park, California, USA
Zhangjiajie National Park, China
Lion Rock, Hong Kong

Also By Andy Fine:

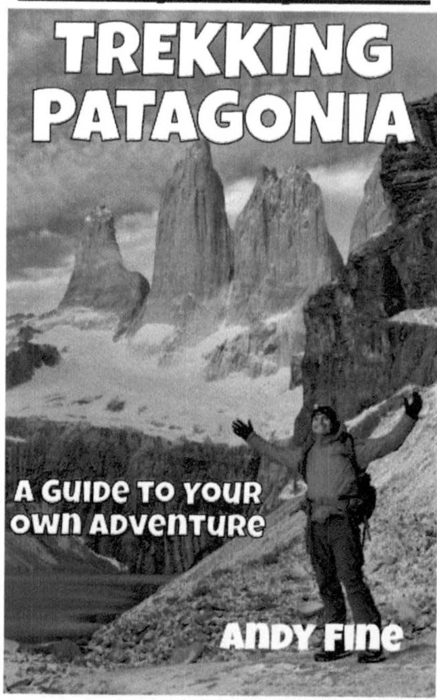

Available on Amazon!

Trekking Patagonia: A Guide to Your Own Adventure tells the story of my three-week backpacking trip to a true hiker's paradise and includes insider information and instruction regarding how to trek the highlights of the area including Torres del Paine National Park, Los Glaciares National Park including El Chaltén and El Calafate, Ushuaia, and Tierra del Fuego. Planning a trip to the bottom of the globe in Patagonia is challenging. Knowing where to go and how much time to spend are just the beginning of planning an adventure to this incredible place. This guidebook will be one of many resources you need to plan your trip. I will give you a great amount of information to help answer some of the confusing questions all travelers to Patagonia will face. With a Pre-Trip Planning Guide, Sample Itineraries, and personally designed overview Trail Maps, this book gives imperative detail and information to help you plan your own adventure. Available on Amazon!

www.ingramcontent.com/pod-product-compliance
Ingram Content Group UK Ltd.
Pitfield, Milton Keynes, MK11 3LW, UK
UKHW041638190726
13854UKWH00006B/2560